Copyright @ 2023 Jessica AcMoody - Elemental Faith Publishing

All rights reserved. No part of this publication may be reproduced, distributed or transmitted in any form or by any means, including photocopying, recording, or other electronic or mechanical methods, without the prior written permission of the publisher, except in case of brief quotations embodied in critical reviews in certain other noncommercial uses permitted by copyright law.

Cover design and illustrations by Ira Baykovska.
Graphic design by Jessica AcMoody.

First printing edition 2023

The Biblical Feasts
And How Jesus Fulfills Them

A Teaching Guide

Jessica AcMoody
Illustrated by Ira Baykovska

Elemental Faith Publishing

Table of Contents

Overview
Introduction..7
The Biblical Feasts..8
Overview of the Feasts..10

The Spring Feasts
Passover and Feast of Unleavened Bread................12
The Seder Plate..21
The Four Cups..24
Ceremonial Washing..27
The Four Cups Continued..28
The Elijah Cup..33
Feast of First Fruits..35
Book Suggestions and Activities...............................38

The Feast of Weeks
Feast of Weeks...49
Book Suggestions and Activities...............................60

The Fall Feasts
Feast of Trumpets..65
Day of Atonement..72
Feast of Tabernacles..82
Books Suggestions and Activities..............................87

Additional Resources
Connections Between Exodus and Revelation..........90
About the Author and Illustrator................................95
Other Titles by the Author...97

Introduction

There is always a holiday just around the corner and the seasonal commercial offerings shout loudly each time you walk through the grocery store; candy hearts, shamrocks, plastic eggs, chocolate bunnies, pinatas, American flags, pumpkins, turkeys and evergreen trees. Each month or two a new display in stores, a seasonal reminder that another holiday is on the way. Maybe you're like me and something in your heart stirs, you want so much more for your kids than what the commercial symbols of the season offer. You want your kids to know, love and follow Jesus with their whole hearts. As you prayerfully consider what each holiday season will look like for your family, what if you did something new that was actually old and hiding in plain sight? What if you taught your kids about the Biblical feasts and how Jesus fulfills them? I want to invite you to look at Scripture this year in a new way; remembering God's faithfulness to His people Israel and how He perfectly fulfills each of the Biblical feasts in Jesus.

As a former elementary Christian school principal and teacher, I'm always on the hunt for the perfect picture book to teach about a certain topic, season, or holiday. A couple years ago I purchased several picture books about the Biblical feasts for my toddler. I was surprised to find that none taught about how Jesus fulfilled them, so I decided to write a series of children's books on the topic. Teaching our children about the Biblical feasts outlined in Leviticus 23, from a Messianic perspective, is a high priority for our family. And after all God does command His people to celebrate His feasts.

As Gentiles we have the privilege of being invited into God's family, grafted in through the death and resurrection of Jesus, no longer outsiders but adopted in as God's own. While there is no Biblical mandate for Gentiles to celebrate the feasts outlined in Leviticus 23 I personally believe that we do ourselves a monumental disservice if we dismiss our Jewish heritage as we follow a Jewish Messiah. Jesus himself not only celebrated each of these feasts but He himself perfectly fulfills them. I cannot think of a more profound way to truly enter into the rhythms God intended for His people to remember His goodness than by celebrating His feasts year after year.

So, what are the feasts all about? We'll first dive into the Biblical text of Leviticus 23, do a brief overview of each of the feasts and then cover them individually more in-depth. You'll find the illustrations and text from each of the picture books I've written embedded at the beginning of each feast. Enjoy the lyrical text and beautiful illustrations which help make learning about the feasts accessible for the youngest of children, but with the depth that will leave you wanting to dig into God's Word more deeply. Our study will span the Old and New Testament as we look at how God established His feasts and how they find their fulfillment in Jesus. Grab your Bible and the picture books (if you already own them) and let's enjoy going on a journey through history and Scripture together!

*All Scripture references are from the New King James Version

The Biblical Feasts
Leviticus 23

And the Lord spoke to Moses, saying, "Speak to the children of Israel, and say to them: 'The feasts of the Lord, which you shall proclaim to be holy convocations, these are My feasts.

The Sabbath
'Six days shall work be done, but the seventh day is a Sabbath of solemn rest, a holy convocation. You shall do no work on it; it is the Sabbath of the Lord in all your dwellings.

The Passover and Unleavened Bread
'These are the feasts of the Lord, holy convocations which you shall proclaim at their appointed times. On the fourteenth day of the first month at twilight is the Lord's Passover. And on the fifteenth day of the same month is the Feast of Unleavened Bread to the Lord; seven days you must eat unleavened bread. On the first day you shall have a holy convocation; you shall do no customary work on it. But you shall offer an offering made by fire to the Lord for seven days. The seventh day shall be a holy convocation; you shall do no customary work on it.' "

The Feast of Firstfruits
And the Lord spoke to Moses, saying, "Speak to the children of Israel, and say to them: 'When you come into the land which I give to you, and reap its harvest, then you shall bring a sheaf of the firstfruits of your harvest to the priest. He shall wave the sheaf before the Lord, to be accepted on your behalf; on the day after the Sabbath the priest shall wave it. And you shall offer on that day, when you wave the sheaf, a male lamb of the first year, without blemish, as a burnt offering to the Lord. Its grain offering shall be two-tenths of an ephah of fine flour mixed with oil, an offering made by fire to the Lord, for a sweet aroma; and its drink offering shall be of wine, one-fourth of a hin. You shall eat neither bread nor parched grain nor fresh grain until the same day that you have brought an offering to your God; it shall be a statute forever throughout your generations in all your dwellings.

The Feast of Weeks
'And you shall count for yourselves from the day after the Sabbath, from the day that you brought the sheaf of the wave offering: seven Sabbaths shall be completed. Count fifty days to the day after the seventh Sabbath; then you shall offer a new grain offering to the Lord. You shall bring from your dwellings two wave loaves of two-tenths of an ephah. They shall be of fine flour; they shall be baked with leaven. They are the firstfruits to the Lord. And you shall offer with the bread seven lambs of the first year, without blemish, one young bull, and two rams. They shall be as a burnt offering to the Lord, with their grain offering and their drink offerings, an offering made by fire for a sweet aroma to the Lord. Then you shall sacrifice one kid of the goats as a sin offering, and two male lambs of the first year as a sacrifice of a peace offering. The priest shall wave them with the bread of the firstfruits as a wave offering before the Lord, with the two lambs. They shall be holy to the Lord for the priest.

And you shall proclaim on the same day that it is a holy convocation to you. You shall do no customary work on it. It shall be a statute forever in all your dwellings throughout your generations.

'When you reap the harvest of your land, you shall not wholly reap the corners of your field when you reap, nor shall you gather any gleaning from your harvest. You shall leave them for the poor and for the stranger: I am the Lord your God.' "

The Feast of Trumpets
Then the Lord spoke to Moses, saying, "Speak to the children of Israel, saying: 'In the seventh month, on the first day of the month, you shall have a sabbath-rest, a memorial of blowing of trumpets, a holy convocation. You shall do no customary work on it; and you shall offer an offering made by fire to the Lord.'"

The Day of Atonement
And the Lord spoke to Moses, saying: "Also the tenth day of this seventh month shall be the Day of Atonement. It shall be a holy convocation for you; you shall afflict your souls, and offer an offering made by fire to the Lord. And you shall do no work on that same day, for it is the Day of Atonement, to make atonement for you before the Lord your God. For any person who is not afflicted in soul on that same day shall be cut off from his people. And any person who does any work on that same day, that person I will destroy from among his people. You shall do no manner of work; it shall be a statute forever throughout your generations in all your dwellings. It shall be to you a sabbath of solemn rest, and you shall afflict your souls; on the ninth day of the month at evening, from evening to evening, you shall celebrate your sabbath."

The Feast of Tabernacles
Then the Lord spoke to Moses, saying, "Speak to the children of Israel, saying: 'The fifteenth day of this seventh month shall be the Feast of Tabernacles for seven days to the Lord. On the first day there shall be a holy convocation. You shall do no customary work on it. For seven days you shall offer an offering made by fire to the Lord. On the eighth day you shall have a holy convocation, and you shall offer an offering made by fire to the Lord. It is a sacred assembly, and you shall do no customary work on it.

'These are the feasts of the Lord which you shall proclaim to be holy convocations, to offer an offering made by fire to the Lord, a burnt offering and a grain offering, a sacrifice and drink offerings, everything on its day — besides the Sabbaths of the Lord, besides your gifts, besides all your vows, and besides all your freewill offerings which you give to the Lord.

'Also on the fifteenth day of the seventh month, when you have gathered in the fruit of the land, you shall keep the feast of the Lord for seven days; on the first day there shall be a sabbath-rest, and on the eighth day a sabbath-rest. And you shall take for yourselves on the first day the fruit of beautiful trees, branches of palm trees, the boughs of leafy trees, and willows of the brook; and you shall rejoice before the Lord your God for seven days. You shall keep it as a feast to the Lord for seven days in the year. It shall be a statute forever in your generations. You shall celebrate it in the seventh month. You shall dwell in booths for seven days. All who are native Israelites shall dwell in booths, that your generations may know that I made the children of Israel dwell in booths when I brought them out of the land of Egypt: I am the Lord your God.' "

So Moses declared to the children of Israel the feasts of the Lord.

A Brief Overview of the Spring Feasts

Passover
At Passover, we recount the Exodus story, in which God allows His people to endure slavery in Egypt and the suffering they underwent generation after generation in the hands of hard-hearted men, highlighting God's miraculous deliverance from bondage. God sent plagues to change Pharaoh's mind, commanding Pharaoh to "let my people go." Before God sent the final plague, He commanded His people to put the blood of a lamb on each of their doorposts which saved Hebrew families from the death that killed all Egyptian first-born, both man and beast. This moment of salvation for the Hebrew nation points to Jesus, our Passover lamb, and His blood shed for us, to be fully free from the eternal punishment and death that sin brings.

Feast of Unleavened Bread
At the Feast of Unleavened Bread, we recount the quick flight from Egypt to escape the bondage of slavery. God tells His people to take bread without leaven as they leave for the Promised Land since there was no time for bread to rise as they left hastily. The Hebrews are commanded to sweep their houses clean and remove all the leaven. The leaven was a representation of sin that puffed up their hearts. God wanted His people to be free of sin as they entered a new season of relationship with Him. The unleavened bread points to Jesus, the bread of life; perfect, sinless, and His body broken for all of us to fully be free from sin.

Feast of First Fruits
At the Feast of First Fruits, we recount God bringing His people into the Promised Land with its abundance of fruit and crops. God commanded His people to bring the first fruits as an offering to the priest, then the people were finally able to freely worship the Lord, and truly enjoy a time of thanksgiving. The offering of the first fruits points to Jesus' resurrection as He is the "first fruit" risen from the dead. His resurrection points to our final resurrection at the end of the age for all those who choose to follow and obey Him.

Feast of Weeks
At the Feast of Weeks, we recount God giving His people Israel the Torah at Mount Sinai. Jesus came as the fulfillment of the law and then ascended to Heaven. After His ascension Jesus told His disciples to go and wait for the helper from heaven to come. The Holy Spirit was poured out so that God's law could be written on our hearts through relationship with Jesus.

A Brief Overview of the Fall Feasts

Feast of Trumpets

At the Feast of Trumpets or Rosh Hashanah (also called Yom Teruah), we recount God's covenant with His people Israel. God manifests His presence in smoke and fire on Mount Sinai as He came to covenant with His people amidst the sound of a trumpet that caused the people to tremble. The Israelites in turn promised to do everything the Lord commanded them to do. This event would be commemorated year after year by sounding trumpet blasts to remind Israel that they were a people under covenant; a nation who had committed to being God's people.

The Feast of Trumpets will be fully fulfilled when Jesus appears in the sky at the 7th trumpet and "gathers" His Bride. This moment that is to come is our blessed hope as we will be transformed, ready to eternally covenant with Jesus. We long for this moment with hope and anticipation. Jesus will return at the Feast of Trumpets, the Bride will be gathered to meet Him in the air and receive their new bodies, and the Kingdom of God will be inaugurated.

Day of Atonement

On the Day of Atonement or Yom Kippur, we recount Moses coming down from the mountain with the 10 Commandments and finding the Israelites worshipping a golden calf that they had made. In Moses' anger, he breaks the tablets signifying Israel breaking the covenant which the Lord had just made with them. Moses pleads with the Lord to not consume and destroy the Israelites and seeks to make atonement for their sin.

Yom Kippur was the one day each year that the high priest could enter the Holy of Holies to make atonement for the people's sin and ask for God's forgiveness on behalf of all the people of Israel. Throughout the year, the Tabernacle absorbed all the sins of the people in sacrifice after sacrifice, day after day. Yom Kippur is like pushing the "reset" button – cleansing the place from all the sins of the people over the year and going back to zero.

On the final Yom Kippur when Jesus returns, He will remove the sin and iniquity of Israel, and they will look on the One they have pierced. They will mourn and lament and cry out to Him, and He will redeem Israel. Yom Kippur is a beautiful foreshadowing of Jesus. Our great high priest put aside His robes of heavenly splendor and put on human flesh to become one of us.

Feast of Tabernacles

The Feast of Tabernacles, or Sukkot, is a reminder of Israel's wandering in the desert, dwelling in tents. The word sukkot means "tabernacles" or "booths". It is the seventh and final Biblical feast mandated by the Lord and brings completeness. It is a reminder of God's covenant with His people and the future picture of oneness when the Lamb returns and marries His bride.

Passover

Seven feasts in all, God gave His command,
to rest, remember and yearn for His holy land.
As we gaze back in time we'll see God's mighty plan,
and get vision for Jesus, the coming Son of Man.

Each feast of our Lord, is holy and true,
God has a purpose, in each, to include you.
Let's go on a journey, we'll look to the east,
see how God's people celebrated His spring feasts.

In the nation of Egypt a long time ago,
there was a ruler who would not let God's people go.
Trapped in slavery, the people weren't free,
but God told Pharaoh, "You must listen to me!"

God sent plagues to change Pharaoh's mind,
but each time his heart was hard and unkind.
In the final plague God had a secret plan,
to shelter His people and break the pride of this man.

The blood of a lamb on each Hebrew doorpost,
saved God's people from the death that killed most.
Finally, oh finally, God's people were free,
and he led them to safety across the Red Sea.

This special, remarkable story points to Jesus,
God's only Son who came to save each of us.
To free us from sin, that traps us like slaves,
and lead us to walk in new life He displayed.
He's the Passover lamb, blood shed for you and me,
He died and rose again so we could fully be free.

Feast of Unleavened Bread

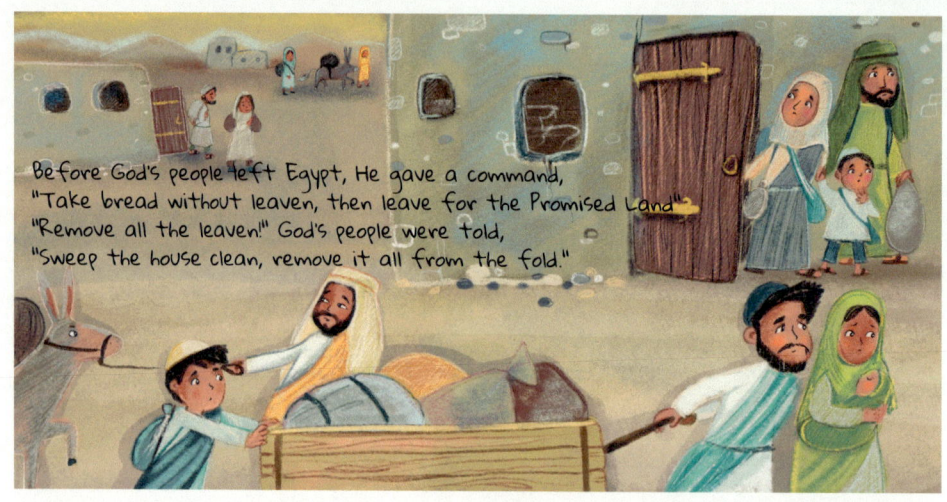

Before God's people left Egypt, He gave a command,
"Take bread without leaven, then leave for the Promised Land."
"Remove all the leaven!" God's people were told,
"Sweep the house clean, remove it all from the fold."

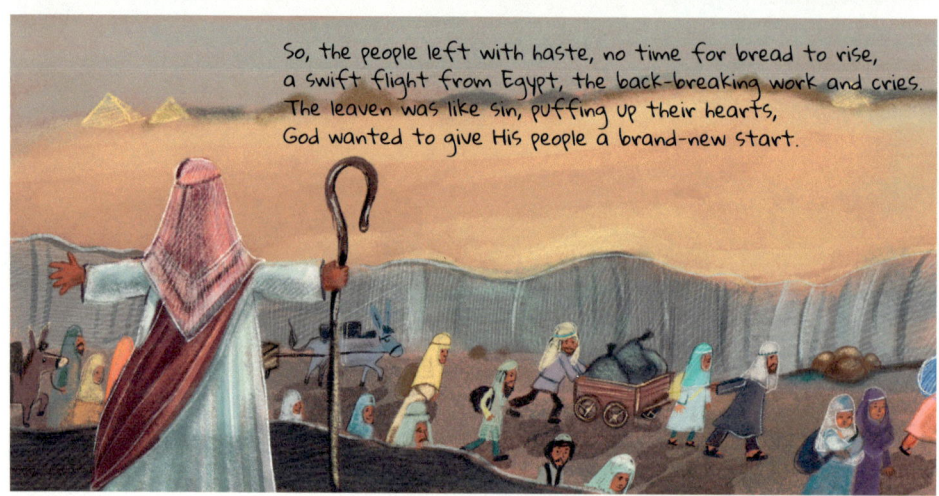

So, the people left with haste, no time for bread to rise,
a swift flight from Egypt, the back-breaking work and cries.
The leaven was like sin, puffing up their hearts,
God wanted to give His people a brand-new start.

For God's people this special moment in time
points towards Jesus who descended from Jesse's line.
Jesus, bread of life, His body broken for all,
freedom for us, no more sin - our downfall.

Matthew 1:1-17

Abraham — Isaac — Jacob — Judah — Perez — Hezron — Ram — Amminadab — Nahshon — Salmon — Boaz — Obed — Jesse — David — Solomon — Rehoboam — Abijah — Asa — Jehoshaphat — Joram — Uzziaz — Jotham — Ahaz — Hezekiah — Manasseh — Amon — Josiah — Jeconiah — Shealtiel — Zerubbabel — Abiud — Eliakim — Azor — Zadok — Achim — Eliud — Matthey — Jacob — Joseph — Mary — Jesus

14

What is Passover and the Feast of Unleavened Bread?

The Passover story takes place in the book of Exodus. For the sake of brevity I am not including the entire text leading up to the Passover story in this the teaching guide. However, I would highly recommend that you take a day or two to reacquaint yourself with the Exodus story and read or listen to Exodus 1-11 before reading further through this teaching guide. The text from these fifteen chapters will likely be familiar and it will be valuable to have the Exodus story fresh in your mind as you read further in this guide. As you read God's Word and this guide consider how to teach the praise-worthy truths of the Lord's salvation of His people and how they are fulfilled through Jesus to your children.

Deuteronomy 6:1-9 is a beautiful summary of the aim of this teaching guide:

"Now this is the commandment, and these are the statutes and judgments which the Lord your God has commanded to teach you, that you may observe them in the land which you are crossing over to possess, that you may fear the Lord your God, to keep all His statutes and His commandments which I command you, you and your son and your grandson, all the days of your life, and that your days may be prolonged. Therefore hear, O Israel, and be careful to observe it, that it may be well with you, and that you may multiply greatly as the Lord God of your fathers has promised you—'a land flowing with milk and honey.'

"Hear, O Israel: The Lord our God, the Lord is one! You shall love the Lord your God with all your heart, with all your soul, and with all your strength.

"And these words which I command you today shall be in your heart. You shall teach them diligently to your children, and shall talk of them when you sit in your house, when you walk by the way, when you lie down, and when you rise up. You shall bind them as a sign on your hand, and they shall be as frontlets between your eyes. You shall write them on the doorposts of your house and on your gates."

As you've read Exodus 1-11 you've remembered how God allowed His people to endure slavery in Egypt, suffering generation after generation in the hands of hard-hearted men. You've recounted each of the plagues God sent to change Pharaoh's mind. Let's now take a look at Exodus 12 when God establishes the Passover and releases the final plague on the Egyptians.

Exodus 12

"Now the Lord spoke to Moses and Aaron in the land of Egypt, saying, "This month shall be your beginning of months; it shall be the first month of the year to you. Speak to all the congregation of Israel, saying: 'On the tenth of this month every man shall take for himself a lamb, according to the house of his father, a lamb for a household. And if the household is too small for the lamb, let him and his neighbor next to his house take it according to the number of the persons; according to each man's need you shall make your count for the lamb. Your lamb shall be without blemish, a male of the first year. You may take it from the sheep or from the goats. Now you shall keep it until the fourteenth day of the same month. Then the whole assembly of the congregation of Israel shall kill it at twilight. And they shall take some of the blood and put it on the two doorposts and on the lintel of the houses where they eat it. Then they shall eat the flesh on that night; roasted in fire, with unleavened bread and with bitter herbs they shall eat it. Do not eat it raw, nor boiled at all with water, but roasted in fire—its head with its legs and its entrails. You shall let none of it remain until morning, and what remains of it until morning you shall burn with fire. And thus you shall eat it: with a belt on your waist, your sandals on your feet, and your staff in your hand. So you shall eat it in haste. It is the Lord's Passover.

'For I will pass through the land of Egypt on that night, and will strike all the firstborn in the land of Egypt, both man and beast; and against all the gods of Egypt I will execute judgment: I am the Lord. Now the blood shall be a sign for you on the houses where you are. And when I see the blood, I will pass over you; and the plague shall not be on you to destroy you when I strike the land of Egypt.

'So this day shall be to you a memorial; and you shall keep it as a feast to the Lord throughout your generations. You shall keep it as a feast by an everlasting ordinance. Seven days you shall eat unleavened bread. On the first day you shall remove leaven from your houses. For whoever eats leavened bread from the first day until the seventh day, that person shall be cut off from Israel. On the first day there shall be a holy convocation, and on the seventh day there shall be a holy convocation for you. No manner of work shall be done on them; but that which everyone must eat—that only may be prepared by you. So you shall observe the Feast of Unleavened Bread, for on this same day I will have brought your armies out of the land of Egypt. Therefore you shall observe this day throughout your generations as an everlasting ordinance."

In the first month, on the fourteenth day of the month at evening, you shall eat unleavened bread, until the twenty-first day of the month at evening. For seven days no leaven shall be found in your houses, since whoever eats what is leavened, that same person shall be cut off from the congregation of Israel, whether he is a stranger or a native of the land. You shall eat nothing leavened; in all your dwellings you shall eat unleavened bread.'

Then Moses called for all the elders of Israel and said to them, "Pick out and take lambs for yourselves according to your families, and kill the Passover lamb. And you shall take a bunch of hyssop, dip it in the blood that is in the basin, and strike the lintel and the two doorposts with the blood that is in the basin. And none of you shall go out of the door of his house until morning. For the Lord will pass through to strike the Egyptians; and when He sees the blood on the lintel and on the two doorposts, the Lord will pass over the door and not allow the destroyer to come into your houses to strike you. And you shall observe this thing as an ordinance for you and your sons forever. It will come to pass when you come to the land which the Lord will give you, just as He promised, that you shall keep this service. And it shall be, when your children say to you, 'What do you mean by this service?' that you shall say, 'It is the Passover sacrifice of the Lord, who passed over the houses of the children of Israel in Egypt when He struck the Egyptians and delivered our households.' " So the people bowed their heads and worshiped. Then the children of Israel went away and did so; just as the Lord had commanded Moses and Aaron, so they did.

And it came to pass at midnight that the Lord struck all the firstborn in the land of Egypt, from the firstborn of Pharaoh who sat on his throne to the firstborn of the captive who was in the dungeon, and all the firstborn of livestock. So Pharaoh rose in the night, he, all his servants, and all the Egyptians; and there was a great cry in Egypt, for there was not a house where there was not one dead.

Then he called for Moses and Aaron by night, and said, "Rise, go out from among my people, both you and the children of Israel. And go, serve the Lord as you have said. Also take your flocks and your herds, as you have said, and be gone; and bless me also."

And the Egyptians urged the people, that they might send them out of the land in haste. For they said, "We shall all be dead." So the people took their dough before it was leavened, having their kneading bowls bound up in their clothes on their shoulders.

Now the children of Israel had done according to the word of Moses, and they had asked from the Egyptians articles of silver, articles of gold, and clothing. And the Lord had given the people favor in the sight of the Egyptians, so that they granted them what they requested. Thus they plundered the Egyptians.

Then the children of Israel journeyed from Rameses to Succoth, about six hundred thousand men on foot, besides children. A mixed multitude went up with them also, and flocks and herds—a great deal of livestock. And they baked unleavened cakes of the dough which they had brought out of Egypt; for it was not leavened, because they were driven out of Egypt and could not wait, nor had they prepared provisions for themselves.

Now the sojourn of the children of Israel who lived in Egypt was four hundred and thirty years. And it came to pass at the end of the four hundred and thirty years—on that very same day—it came to pass that all the armies of the Lord went out from the land of Egypt. It is a night of solemn observance to the Lord for bringing them out of the land of Egypt. This is that night of the Lord, a solemn observance for all the children of Israel throughout their generations.

And the Lord said to Moses and Aaron, "This is the ordinance of the Passover: No foreigner shall eat it. But every man's servant who is bought for money, when you have circumcised him, then he may eat it. A sojourner and a hired servant shall not eat it. In one house it shall be eaten; you shall not carry any of the flesh outside the house, nor shall you break one of its bones. All the congregation of Israel shall keep it. And when a stranger dwells with you and wants to keep the Passover to the Lord, let all his males be circumcised, and then let him come near and keep it; and he shall be as a native of the land. For no uncircumcised person shall eat it. One law shall be for the native-born and for the stranger who dwells among you."

Thus all the children of Israel did; as the Lord commanded Moses and Aaron, so they did. And it came to pass, on that very same day, that the Lord brought the children of Israel out of the land of Egypt according to their armies."

Now we are going to jump to the New Testament, and as you read the story of The Last Supper keep the image of the blood of the lamb and the unleavened bread in your mind. You'll see how the Passover feast, which the Lord institutes in Exodus, is fulfilled in Jesus.

Luke 22:1-21

Then came the Day of Unleavened Bread, when the Passover must be killed. And He sent Peter and John, saying, "Go and prepare the Passover for us, that we may eat."

So they said to Him, "Where do You want us to prepare?"

And He said to them, "Behold, when you have entered the city, a man will meet you carrying a pitcher of water; follow him into the house which he enters. Then you shall say to the master of the house, 'The Teacher says to you, "Where is the guest room where I may eat the Passover with My disciples?" ' Then he will show you a large, furnished upper room; there make ready."

So they went and found it just as He had said to them, and they prepared the Passover.

When the hour had come, He sat down, and the twelve apostles with Him. Then He said to them, "With fervent desire I have desired to eat this Passover with you before I suffer; for I say to you, I will no longer eat of it until it is fulfilled in the kingdom of God."

Then He took the cup, and gave thanks, and said, "Take this and divide it among yourselves; for I say to you, I will not drink of the fruit of the vine until the kingdom of God comes."

And He took bread, gave thanks and broke it, and gave it to them, saying, "This is My body which is given for you; do this in remembrance of Me."

Likewise He also took the cup after supper, saying, "This cup is the new covenant in My blood, which is shed for you. But behold, the hand of My betrayer is with Me on the table."

This moment that Jesus shares with His disciples was in the context of a Passover Seder, a meal that lasted several hours and had deep significance as bread was broken and glasses of wine poured and drank. This is a stark contrast from the short moment of communion many of us have become accustomed to in our churches. In just a moment we'll take an in-depth look at some of the elements of the Passover Seder. But before that let's talk about leaven. Leaven was a type of yeast used in dough to make it rise. Biblically, leaven is used as an analogy for sin or being "puffed up." In Jewish culture, in the days leading up to Passover, the people do a deep cleaning of their homes, and part of the cleaning involves removing any leaven or foods containing leaven from the home.

Jesus purged the leaven after His triumphal entry on Palm Sunday to prepare for Passover by cleansing His Father's house:

Then Jesus went into the temple of God and drove out all those who bought and sold in the temple, and overturned the tables of the money changers and the seats of those who sold doves. And He said to them, "It is written, 'My house shall be called a house of prayer,' but you have made it a 'den of thieves.' " Matthew 21:12-13

As followers of Jesus we can take this practice to heart in a more spiritual sense, removing the leaven from our hearts as we ask the Holy Spirit to reveal sin in our lives. Take a look at what Paul has to say about leaven:

"Therefore purge out the old leaven, that you may be a new lump, since you truly are unleavened. For indeed Christ, our Passover, was sacrificed for us. Therefore let us keep the feast, not with old leaven, nor with the leaven of malice and wickedness, but with the unleavened bread of sincerity and truth." 1 Corinthians 5:7-8

Paul exhorts believers to purge the old leaven so that we might be a new lump. This analogy refers to our new life that we have through Jesus and the ongoing journey of sanctification as the Holy Spirit works in us. Passover is a time where we can intentionally search our hearts asking the Lord to reveal sin and by the power of the Holy Spirit ask Him to cleanse us anew because of the blood of the Lamb. Likewise we are to examine ourselves before the Lord as we remember His sacrifice as the Passover lamb.

"Therefore whoever eats this bread or drinks this cup of the Lord in an unworthy manner will be guilty of the body and blood of the Lord. But let a man examine himself, and so let him eat of the bread and drink of the cup. For he who eats and drinks in an unworthy manner eats and drinks judgment to himself, not discerning the Lord's body." 1 Corinthians 11:27-29

Now let's return to the Passover Seder, the original context that communion would have been taken in. The seder would have been a meal that spanned several hours, portions of Scripture would be read and sometimes acted out, different elements on the seder plate were referred to each pointing to part of the Exodus story, glasses of wine drank and questions asked. It was an evening of rich history and remembering the mercy and goodness of the Lord to His people Israel.

The Seder Plate

Let's take a look at some of the specific elements on the Seder plate and the scriptural significance of each:

Parsley & Salt Water: The parsley on the Seder plate represents life, specifically the life of God's people Israel which began as a tiny seed. The Lord "planted" His people in Egypt via Jacob (see Genesis 37-50 for a full history). There in Egypt God's people grew into a mighty nation (see Exodus 1). God then used Moses to lead His people out of slavery, giving them "new life" as He brought them into the wilderness and eventually the promised land. When we first meet Christ our faith is like a tiny seed planted that brings us out of slavery and into His eternal promised land. The salt water represents the tears shed over the hardship of slavery that God's people endured in Egypt as well as their deliverance as they were led to freedom through the parting of the Red Sea (Exodus 14). As followers of Christ we can identify with tears shed in repentance over our sin. As we submit and surrender to the deliverance Jesus brings to our lives, we too are led into freedom from our former bondage of sin.

Lettuce/Bitter Herbs: The bitter herbs on the Seder plate, typically romaine lettuce, represent the bitterness of slavery in Egypt (see Exodus 1). As followers of Christ, we can identify with the bitterness of sin when we were once held captive and in bondage, slaves to sin.

Charoset: The charoset on the Seder plate is a mixture of chopped apples with walnut and cinnamon, a reminder of the mortar used in Egypt to build; but amidst turmoil there was sweetness (see Exodus 1). As followers of Christ we can identify with the sweetness that Jesus brings into our lives amidst hardship and tumultuous circumstances. During the Seder, the lettuce is dipped into the charoset a beautiful reminder that God sees us in the midst of our struggle and has a plan to redeem all things.

Roasted Egg: The egg on the Seder plate symbolizes new life as Passover is the beginning of the new year. The egg itself is never referenced during the Passover Seder however it is referenced in rabbinic Jewish texts and is thought to be a substitute for the roasted lamb as the traditional sacrifice. Eating an egg is a sign of mourning and in Jewish tradition the first food eaten after a funeral. This could be a connection to the mourning of the Jewish people as they no longer offer an animal sacrifice at Passover due to the lack of a physical temple in Jerusalem. As believers in Christ we can see the roasted egg and mourn with our Jewish brothers and sisters that they do not yet see the fullness of new life that Jesus brings and pray for the veil to be removed from their eyes.

Matzah: The matzah, or unleavened bread, represents Jesus the Messiah who "knew no sin". If you look at a traditional piece of matzah you will see the bread is both stripped and pierced giving it a bruised appearance. Consider the matzah and the description of the "Sin-Bearing Messiah" in Isaiah 53:4-5:

"Surely He has borne our griefs and carried our sorrows; yet we esteemed Him stricken, smitten by God, and afflicted. But He was wounded for our transgressions, He was bruised for our iniquities; the chastisement for our peace was upon Him, and by His stripes we are healed."

Traditionally during the Seder meal the leader had three pieces of matzah stacked; this is referred to as "the unity". Historically "the unity" had a multifaceted meaning; the unity of the patriarchs (Abraham, Isaac and Jacob), the unity of the Israelites (priests, Levites and the rest of the people) or the unity of the trinity (Father, Son and Spirit). The leader takes the stacked matzah, removes the middle matzah and breaks it in half, representing Jesus body broken for us. The broken matzah is then wrapped in a cloth and "buried". This piece of matzah becomes the afikomen which someone hides and the guests search for later; the one who finds the hidden afikomen receives a prize. When the afikomen is found it is then given to the leader who then reunites it with the other half of the broken matzah. What was broken is made whole. Through Jesus's sacrifice, we are made whole. The leader then breaks off small pieces of the afikomen to distribute to all. Recall Jesus' words to His disciples during the Passover feast:

"And He took bread, gave thanks and broke it, and gave it to them, saying, "This is My body which is given for you; do this in remembrance of Me."" Luke 22:19

Prior to the search for the afikomen, the leader of the Seder breaks off a piece of the bottom matzah and dips it in horseradish, a symbol of the growing oppression of slavery in Egypt over time and the hope of deliverance growing dim. As everyone present at the Seder dips a piece from the bottom matzah in the horseradish the suffering of God's people is commemorated.

Shank Bone: The shank bone on the Seder plate represents the Passover lamb which was sacrificed as a covering for the Israelites, a beautiful parallel to Jesus our Passover lamb sacrificed for us. When the blood of the lamb was applied to the doorpost in the Passover story it was painted on in the sign of a cross, another foreshadowing of Jesus' blood poured out on the cross.

Passover lambs had specific requirements (see Exodus 12:5-6); without blemish, male, "one year old" (a Hebrew phrase for pure) and would have been kept for a time of observation before being sacrificed. When sacrificed, none of their bones could be broken. This also parallels the life of Jesus: He was without blemish, male, "one year" (pure), would have been observed by many during His years of ministry before being sacrificed, and when crucified, none of His bones were broken.

A couple other significant parallels between the Passover lambs and Jesus include the location where they were born and how they were brought into Jerusalem.

Passover lambs were born and bred right outside of Jerusalem in Bethlehem and they were brought into Jerusalem through the sheep gate the same gate Jesus entered through on Palm Sunday. When the Passover lambs were brought into Jerusalem there was great rejoicing as the sacrifice came into the city. Likewise recall the great rejoicing that occurred on Palm Sunday as Jesus entered the city of Jerusalem:

"The next day a great multitude that had come to the feast, when they heard that Jesus was coming to Jerusalem, took branches of palm trees and went out to meet Him, and cried out: "Hosanna! 'Blessed is He who comes in the name of the Lord!' The King of Israel!'" John 12:12-13

Finally the time of the day in which the Passover lambs were sacrificed was perfectly fulfilled in Jesus' death on the cross. According to Exodus 12:6, Passover lambs were sacrificed at "twilight;" this word translated means middle of the evening. Jewish days were broken up by the daylight hours; morning (6am - noon) and evening (noon - 6pm). Historically the priest would ascend the altar at 3pm with the Passover lamb as sacrifices were a lengthy process and required to be completed by sundown. Once the lamb was fully prepared another priest would ascend the temple wall and with a blowing of the shofar the lamb's throat would be cut and the sacrifice complete, a shout of "it is finished" would be declared. Let's take a look at Luke 23:44-46 and how Jesus' death on the cross fulfills the Passover sacrifice:

"Now it was about the sixth hour, and there was darkness over all the earth until the ninth hour. Then the sun was darkened, and the veil of the temple was torn in two. And when Jesus had cried out with a loud voice, He said, "Father, 'into Your hands I commit My spirit.' "Having said this, He breathed His last."

And John 19:30b adds "He said, "It is finished!" And bowing His head, He gave up His spirit."

The Four Cups

Another main element of the Passover Seder is the four cups. Wine was traditionally used; however, if your family does not drink alcohol, or you are wanting a completely kid-friendly option, grape juice can be used. Our church has a Passover Seder yearly and uses grape juice. Each of the four cups is based on the "I will" promises in Exodus 6:6-7 and can also be rooted in additional Scripture from a Messianic standpoint. The cups of wine or grape juice are consumed over the course of the hours of the Seder meal. Let's first read Exodus 6:6-7 before taking a look at each of the cups:

"Therefore say to the children of Israel: 'I am the Lord; I will bring you out from under the burdens of the Egyptians, I will rescue you from their bondage, and I will redeem you with an outstretched arm and with great judgments. I will take you as My people, and I will be your God. Then you shall know that I am the Lord your God who brings you out from under the burdens of the Egyptians."

1 - The Cup of Sanctification "I will bring you out from under the burdens of the Egyptians."

Jesus our Messiah sanctifies us:
"And for their sakes I sanctify Myself, that they also may be sanctified by the truth." John 17:19 and "But of Him you are in Christ Jesus, who became for us wisdom from God—and righteousness and sanctification and redemption..." 1 Corinthians 1:30

To be sanctified is to be set apart. God sanctified His people Israel and set them apart from the other nations. The Israelites were called by God to live very differently. The Mosaic law outlines all the requirements – 613 ways to live rightly in all! These requirements covered all areas of life: eating, drinking, the way they dressed, washing, daily tasks, religious duties, and sacrifices. Every area of life was covered in some way by the law. The fullness of God's heart was never that the law would make His people holy, but that He himself would sanctify and make them holy. As believers in Jesus, we are grafted into this sanctification. We are however called to live differently and set apart from the world around us. Paul writes of how we are sanctified by the work of the Holy Spirit:

"Now I myself am confident concerning you, my brethren, that you also are full of goodness, filled with all knowledge, able also to admonish one another. Nevertheless, brethren, I have written more boldly to you on some points, as reminding you, because of the grace given to me by God, that I might be a minister of Jesus Christ to the Gentiles, ministering the gospel of God, that the offering of the Gentiles might be acceptable, sanctified by the Holy Spirit. Therefore I have reason to glory in Christ Jesus in the things which pertain to God." Romans 15:15-17

Consider God's heart for all peoples and nations to be set apart and have a place in His house:

Thus says the Lord: "Keep justice, and do righteousness, for My salvation is about to come, and My righteousness to be revealed. Blessed is the man who does this, and the son of man who lays hold on it; who keeps from defiling the Sabbath, and keeps his hand from doing any evil."

Do not let the son of the foreigner who has joined himself to the Lord speak, saying, "The Lord has utterly separated me from His people"; nor let the eunuch say, "Here I am, a dry tree." For thus says the Lord: "To the eunuchs who keep My Sabbaths, and choose what pleases Me, and hold fast My covenant, even to them I will give in My house and within My walls a place and a name better than that of sons and daughters; I will give them an everlasting name that shall not be cut off.

"Also the sons of the foreigner who join themselves to the Lord, to serve Him, and to love the name of the Lord, to be His servants— Everyone who keeps from defiling the Sabbath, and holds fast My covenant— Even them I will bring to My holy mountain, and make them joyful in My house of prayer. Their burnt offerings and their sacrifices will be accepted on My altar; for My house shall be called a house of prayer for all nations." The Lord God, who gathers the outcasts of Israel, says, "Yet I will gather to him others besides those who are gathered to him." Isaiah 56:1-8

In Jesus, all are welcome to enter into the sanctification that He offers through the regenerative work of the Holy Spirit. Grafted in, we share in the inheritance God had set apart for His people Israel.

2- The Cup of Deliverance "I will rescue you from bondage"

Jesus our Messiah delivers us, John 8:32:
"And you shall know the truth, and the truth shall make you free."

"For when you were slaves of sin, you were free in regard to righteousness. What fruit did you have then in the things of which you are now ashamed? For the end of those things is death. But now having been set free from sin, and having become slaves of God, you have your fruit to holiness, and the end, everlasting life. For the wages of sin is death, but the gift of God is eternal life in Christ Jesus our Lord." Romans 6:20-23

In the Passover Seder, this cup is filled to the brim. The cup of deliverance is also known as the cup of judgment. The full cup symbolizes complete joy through the fullness of God's judgments. Through the plagues brought against the Egyptians, God brought about the deliverance of the Israelites. So too, God's judgments in the last days will bring about the deliverance of His people, both Jew and Gentile preceding His final return. We'll get into that more in a bit. Let's first take a look at the judgments or plagues God sent upon the Egyptians. Head on over to Exodus 7-11 in your Bible and read or listen to these chapters with an audio Bible.

During the Passover Seder, each of the plagues is referenced. Everyone dips a finger in the cup and the wine or juice is sprinkled on a plate while each person says the name of each plague, repeating them three times: "blood, blood, blood" as the juice is sprinkled on the plate "frogs, frogs, frogs" and again the juice is sprinkled. This continues through all 10 plagues.

Often we think of judgment in a negative light but God intends for His judgment to be desired by believers. The judgments of the Lord are righteous and are also His mercy. Consider what David says in Psalm 19:

"The fear of the LORD is clean, enduring forever; the judgments of the LORD are true and righteous altogether. More to be desired are they than gold, yea, than much fine gold; sweeter also than honey and the honeycomb. Moreover by them Your servant is warned, and in keeping them there is great reward." Psalm 19:9-11

Praise God that the deliverance of His people was a beautiful foreshadowing of the deliverance that Christ brings to us now, and also points to the final deliverance of His people at the end of the age. If you'd like to learn a bit more about the connections between the Exodus judgments and the judgments in Revelation at the end of days, see the "Connections Between Exodus and Revelation" at the back of this teaching guide.

"For Christ also suffered once for sins, the just for the unjust, that He might bring us to God, being put to death in the flesh but made alive by the Spirit..." 1 Peter 3:18

Ceremonial Washing

Typically between the second and third cup of the Passover Seder there is a ceremonial washing of the hands. This is a beautiful illustration of Jesus washing His disciples feet at the Last Supper. The one who was the most honored guest at the Passover seder was taking the position of lowliness and humility. Historically feet would have gotten extremely dusty walking the dirt roads and it would have been the role of a servant of wash the feet of guests that came to a home. Jesus models what serving one another should look like, being willing to take the position of lowliness and humility.

"Now before the Feast of the Passover, when Jesus knew that His hour had come that He should depart from this world to the Father, having loved His own who were in the world, He loved them to the end.

And supper being ended, the devil having already put it into the heart of Judas Iscariot, Simon's son, to betray Him, Jesus, knowing that the Father had given all things into His hands, and that He had come from God and was going to God, rose from supper and laid aside His garments, took a towel and girded Himself. After that, He poured water into a basin and began to wash the disciples' feet, and to wipe them with the towel with which He was girded. Then He came to Simon Peter. And Peter said to Him, "Lord, are You washing my feet?"

Jesus answered and said to him, "What I am doing you do not understand now, but you will know after this." Peter said to Him, "You shall never wash my feet!" Jesus answered him, "If I do not wash you, you have no part with Me." Simon Peter said to Him, "Lord, not my feet only, but also my hands and my head!"

Jesus said to him, "He who is bathed needs only to wash his feet, but is completely clean; and you are clean, but not all of you." For He knew who would betray Him; therefore He said, "You are not all clean."

So when He had washed their feet, taken His garments, and sat down again, He said to them, "Do you know what I have done to you? You call Me Teacher and Lord, and you say well, for so I am. If I then, your Lord and Teacher, have washed your feet, you also ought to wash one another's feet. For I have given you an example, that you should do as I have done to you. Most assuredly, I say to you, a servant is not greater than his master; nor is he who is sent greater than he who sent him. If you know these things, blessed are you if you do them." John 13:1-17

The Four Cups Continued...

3 - The Cup of Redemption
"I will redeem you with an outstretched arm and with great judgments."

Jesus our Messiah redeems us, Galatians 3:13-14: (a reference to Deuteronomy 21:22-23)
"Christ has redeemed us from the curse of the law, having become a curse for us (for it is written, "Cursed is everyone who hangs on a tree"), that the blessing of Abraham might come upon the Gentiles in Christ Jesus, that we might receive the promise of the Spirit through faith."

But when the fullness of the time had come, God sent forth His Son, born of a woman, born under the law, to redeem those who were under the law, that we might receive the adoption as sons." Galatians 4:4-5

Preceding the crucifixion, in the context of the Passover Seder Jesus eludes to what He will do and asks His disciples to "remember." Imagine their surprise considering what would unfold over the next 24 hours. Recall Jesus' words in Luke 22:20: "Likewise He also took the cup after supper, saying, "This cup is the new covenant in My blood, which is shed for you."

Historically, wine would have been a 50/50 mixture of the wine itself and water. The words of Jesus, "my blood shed for you," bring a whole new meaning to the piercing of Jesus' side in John 19:34 "But when they came to Jesus and saw that He was already dead, they did not break His legs. But one of the soldiers pierced His side with a spear, and immediately blood and water came out."

The mixture that came out when Jesus was pierced was blood and water, just like the cup Jesus held up for his disciples as He instituted the New Covenant. Medically speaking the blood and water flowing out was evidence of the excruciating pain Jesus endured and the pressure on His body, His heart exploding. The blood would have settled and the water would have separated from it, causing both blood and water to flow out when his side was pierced. Jesus' cause of physical death was a broken heart. What a fitting analogy as we consider the weight of all sin and iniquity put on Jesus at the cross, and His feelings of abandonment by the Father.

"And about the ninth hour Jesus cried out with a loud voice, saying, "Eli, Eli, lama sabachthani?" that is, "My God, My God, why have You forsaken Me?"" Matthew 27:46

Jesus knew well the intense pain he would endure on the cross and even prayed to the Father during His final hours that, "this cup might pass from me, but not my will but yours."

Then Jesus came with them to a place called Gethsemane, and said to the disciples, "Sit here while I go and pray over there." And He took with Him Peter and the two sons of Zebedee, and He began to be sorrowful and deeply distressed. Then He said to them, "My soul is exceedingly sorrowful, even to death. Stay here and watch with Me."

He went a little farther and fell on His face, and prayed, saying, "O My Father, if it is possible, let this cup pass from Me; nevertheless, not as I will, but as You will."

Then He came to the disciples and found them sleeping, and said to Peter, "What! Could you not watch with Me one hour? Watch and pray, lest you enter into temptation. The spirit indeed is willing, but the flesh is weak."

Again, a second time, He went away and prayed, saying, "O My Father, if this cup cannot pass away from Me unless I drink it, Your will be done." And He came and found them asleep again, for their eyes were heavy.

So He left them, went away again, and prayed the third time, saying the same words. Then He came to His disciples and said to them, "Are you still sleeping and resting? Behold, the hour is at hand, and the Son of Man is being betrayed into the hands of sinners. Rise, let us be going. See, My betrayer is at hand." Matthew 26:36-46

Consider again Isaiah's description of the sin bearing Messiah in light of the cup of redemption:

"Surely He has borne our griefs and carried our sorrows; yet we esteemed Him stricken, smitten by God, and afflicted. But He was wounded for our transgressions, He was bruised for our iniquities; the chastisement for our peace was upon Him, and by His stripes we are healed. All we like sheep have gone astray; we have turned, every one, to his own way; and the Lord has laid on Him the iniquity of us all." Isaiah 53:4-6

Praise Jesus that His blood was poured out, and His heart was broken and pierced for our redemption.

4 - The Cup of Praise or Completion "I will take you as my people, and I will be your God."

Jesus our Messiah is our joy and the completion of God's plan. Read John 15:1-17:
"I am the true vine, and My Father is the vinedresser. Every branch in Me that does not bear fruit He takes away; and every branch that bears fruit He prunes, that it may bear more fruit. You are already clean because of the word which I have spoken to you. Abide in Me, and I in you. As the branch cannot bear fruit of itself, unless it abides in the vine, neither can you, unless you abide in Me.

"I am the vine, you are the branches. He who abides in Me, and I in him, bears much fruit; for without Me you can do nothing. If anyone does not abide in Me, he is cast out as a branch and is withered; and they gather them and throw them into the fire, and they are burned. If you abide in Me, and My words abide in you, you will ask what you desire, and it shall be done for you. By this My Father is glorified, that you bear much fruit; so you will be My disciples.

"As the Father loved Me, I also have loved you; abide in My love. If you keep My commandments, you will abide in My love, just as I have kept My Father's commandments and abide in His love.

"These things I have spoken to you, that My joy may remain in you, and that your joy may be full. This is My commandment, that you love one another as I have loved you. Greater love has no one than this, than to lay down one's life for his friends. You are My friends if you do whatever I command you. No longer do I call you servants, for a servant does not know what his master is doing; but I have called you friends, for all things that I heard from My Father I have made known to you. You did not choose Me, but I chose you and appointed you that you should go and bear fruit, and that your fruit should remain, that whatever you ask the Father in My name He may give you. These things I command you, that you love one another."

The cup of praise is also known as the cup of completion. Jesus alludes to this completion in Mark 14:25: "Assuredly, I say to you, I will no longer drink of the fruit of the vine until that day when I drink it new in the kingdom of God." Jesus himself did not drink of the fourth cup during the Passover Seder although His disciples would have.

What a celebration and feast that will be when we drink of the marriage wine in the New Jerusalem at the marriage feast of the Lamb and His Bride!

"Let us be glad and rejoice and give Him glory, for the marriage of the Lamb has come, and His wife has made herself ready." And to her it was granted to be arrayed in fine linen, clean and bright, for the fine linen is the righteous acts of the saints. Then he said to me, "Write: 'Blessed are those who are called to the marriage supper of the Lamb!' " And he said to me, "These are the true sayings of God."" Revelation 19:7-9

The Seder traditionally concludes with the singing of Psalms 115-118; "And when they had sung a hymn, they went out to the Mount of Olives." Matthew 26:30. **Consider the words of Psalm 118 right before Jesus goes into the Garden of Gethsemane:**

"Oh, give thanks to the Lord, for He is good! For His mercy endures forever. Let Israel now say, "His mercy endures forever." Let the house of Aaron now say, "His mercy endures forever." Let those who fear the Lord now say, "His mercy endures forever."

I called on the Lord in distress; the Lord answered me and set me in a broad place. The Lord is on my side; I will not fear. What can man do to me? The Lord is for me among those who help me; therefore I shall see my desire on those who hate me.

It is better to trust in the Lord than to put confidence in man. It is better to trust in the Lord than to put confidence in princes. All nations surrounded me, but in the name of the Lord I will destroy them. They surrounded me, yes, they surrounded me; but in the name of the Lord I will destroy them.

They surrounded me like bees; they were quenched like a fire of thorns; for in the name of the Lord I will destroy them. You pushed me violently, that I might fall, but the Lord helped me. The Lord is my strength and song, and He has become my salvation.

The voice of rejoicing and salvation is in the tents of the righteous; the right hand of the Lord does valiantly. The right hand of the Lord is exalted; the right hand of the Lord does valiantly. I shall not die, but live, and declare the works of the Lord. The Lord has chastened me severely, but He has not given me over to death.

Open to me the gates of righteousness; I will go through them, and I will praise the Lord. This is the gate of the Lord, through which the righteous shall enter. I will praise You, for You have answered me, and have become my salvation.

The stone which the builders rejected has become the chief cornerstone. This was the Lord's doing; it is marvelous in our eyes. This is the day the Lord has made; we will rejoice and be glad in it. Save now, I pray, O Lord; O Lord, I pray, send now prosperity. Blessed is he who comes in the name of the Lord! We have blessed you from the house of the Lord.

God is the Lord, and He has given us light; bind the sacrifice with cords to the horns of the altar. You are my God, and I will praise You; you are my God, I will exalt You. Oh, give thanks to the Lord, for He is good! For His mercy endures forever."

The Elijah Cup

One tradition embedded in the Passover Seder is the role of Elijah. A cup is set at the table in His honor and there is even a part of the Seder where a door is opened to see if Elijah is there. Tradition holds that Elijah will return just before the coming of the Messiah during Passover. Recall from Scripture how Elijah was taken to heaven as well as how Scripture prophesies his spirit through John the Baptist, a forerunner of Jesus. Read 2 Kings 2:1-11 and then consider the role of John the Baptist:

"Behold, I send My messenger, and he will prepare the way before Me. And the Lord, whom you seek, will suddenly come to His temple, even the Messenger of the covenant, in whom you delight. Behold, He is coming," says the Lord of hosts." Malachi 3:1

"As they departed, Jesus began to say to the multitudes concerning John: "What did you go out into the wilderness to see? A reed shaken by the wind? But what did you go out to see? A man clothed in soft garments? Indeed, those who wear soft clothing are in kings' houses. But what did you go out to see? A prophet? Yes, I say to you, and more than a prophet. For this is he of whom it is written: 'Behold, I send My messenger before Your face, Who will prepare Your way before You.'

"Assuredly, I say to you, among those born of women there has not risen one greater than John the Baptist; but he who is least in the kingdom of heaven is greater than he. And from the days of John the Baptist until now the kingdom of heaven suffers violence, and the violent take it by force. For all the prophets and the law prophesied until John. And if you are willing to receive it, he is Elijah who is to come. He who has ears to hear, let him hear! Matthew 11:7-15

"And His disciples asked Him, saying, "Why then do the scribes say that Elijah must come first?" Jesus answered and said to them, "Indeed, Elijah is coming first and will restore all things. But I say to you that Elijah has come already, and they did not know him but did to him whatever they wished. Likewise the Son of Man is also about to suffer at their hands." Then the disciples understood that He spoke to them of John the Baptist." Matthew 17:10-13

"For he will be great in the sight of the Lord, and shall drink neither wine nor strong drink. He will also be filled with the Holy Spirit, even from his mother's womb. And he will turn many of the children of Israel to the Lord their God. He will also go before Him in the spirit and power of Elijah, 'to turn the hearts of the fathers to the children,' and the disobedient to the wisdom of the just, to make ready a people prepared for the Lord."" Luke 1:15-17

Now consider the role of the spirit of Elijah in the last days:

"Behold, I will send you Elijah the prophet before the coming of the great and dreadful day of the Lord. And he will turn the hearts of the fathers to the children, and the hearts of the children to their fathers, lest I come and strike the earth with a curse." Malachi 4:5-6

The role of the Spirit of Elijah both in the days of John the Baptist and the last days preceding the return of Jesus is to turn the hearts of people to God. Just think of the multitudes upon multitudes that were prepared by John the Baptist to receive Jesus when He came. So too in the last days, the role of the Church is to prepare multitudes upon multitudes for the second coming of Jesus.

Feast of First Fruits

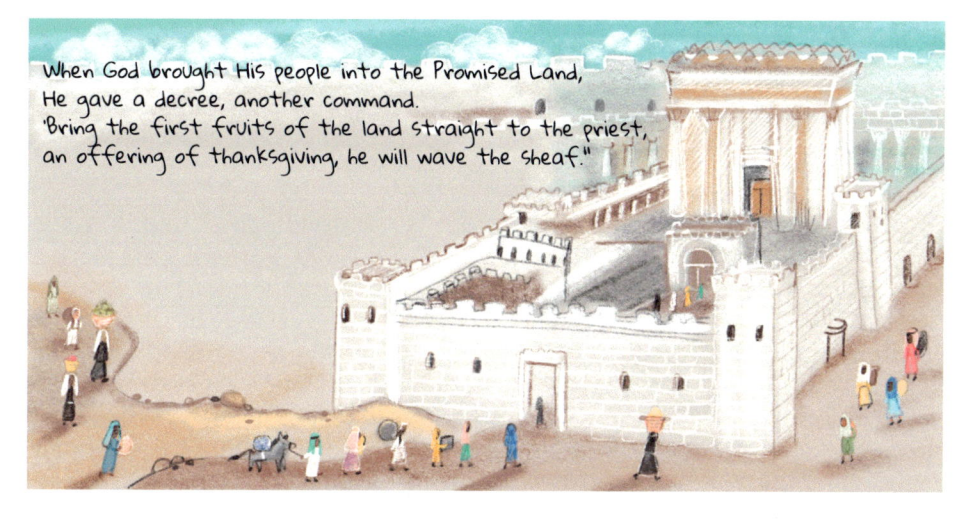

When God brought His people into the Promised Land,
He gave a decree, another command.
"Bring the first fruits of the land straight to the priest,
an offering of thanksgiving, he will wave the sheaf."

Thanksgiving to the Lord for His mighty deeds,
meant offering the first fruits of all crops and trees.
The people were so glad to freely worship the Lord,
with fertile land, crops aplenty, their hearts soared.

Jesus is our first fruit, He rose from the dead,
the promise of eternal life, and resurrection He led.
This Feast of First Fruits points to a great day,
the resurrection of all who trust and obey.

What is the Feast of Firstfruits?

"And the Lord spoke to Moses, saying, "Speak to the children of Israel, and say to them: 'When you come into the land which I give to you, and reap its harvest, then you shall bring a sheaf of the firstfruits of your harvest to the priest. He shall wave the sheaf before the Lord, to be accepted on your behalf; on the day after the Sabbath the priest shall wave it. And you shall offer on that day, when you wave the sheaf, a male lamb of the first year, without blemish, as a burnt offering to the Lord. Its grain offering shall be two-tenths of an ephah of fine flour mixed with oil, an offering made by fire to the Lord, for a sweet aroma; and its drink offering shall be of wine, one-fourth of a hin. You shall eat neither bread nor parched grain nor fresh grain until the same day that you have brought an offering to your God; it shall be a statute forever throughout your generations in all your dwellings." Leviticus 23:9-14

"And it shall be, when you come into the land which the Lord your God is giving you as an inheritance, and you possess it and dwell in it, that you shall take some of the first of all the produce of the ground, which you shall bring from your land that the Lord your God is giving you, and put it in a basket and go to the place where the Lord your God chooses to make His name abide. And you shall go to the one who is priest in those days, and say to him, 'I declare today to the Lord your God that I have come to the country which the Lord swore to our fathers to give us.'

"Then the priest shall take the basket out of your hand and set it down before the altar of the Lord your God. And you shall answer and say before the Lord your God: 'My father was a Syrian, about to perish, and he went down to Egypt and dwelt there, few in number; and there he became a nation, great, mighty, and populous. But the Egyptians mistreated us, afflicted us, and laid hard bondage on us. Then we cried out to the Lord God of our fathers, and the Lord heard our voice and looked on our affliction and our labor and our oppression. So the Lord brought us out of Egypt with a mighty hand and with an outstretched arm, with great terror and with signs and wonders. He has brought us to this place and has given us this land, "a land flowing with milk and honey"; and now, behold, I have brought the first-fruits of the land which you, O Lord, have given me.' Deuteronomy 26:1-10

Following tradition on the first day of Passover farmers went out to survey their harvest, looking for the buds that sprang up first. There would be special ribbons used to mark those buds. Then on the third day of Passover the farmer would again survey the harvest and see which of the buds marked were ready to be harvested. Those buds ready to be harvested would be cut immediately, taken to the temple to be presented and waved before the Lord as Scripture commands.

God's command to the Israelites in both Leviticus and Deuteronomy is a foreshadowing of Jesus, our firstfruit, resurrected from the dead. Jesus through His resurrection has made a way for us to dwell in His eternal promised land as He gives us victory over sin and death.

"But now Christ is risen from the dead, and has become the firstfruits of those who have fallen asleep. For since by man came death, by Man also came the resurrection of the dead. For as in Adam all die, even so in Christ all shall be made alive. But each one in his own order: Christ the firstfruits, afterward those who are Christ's at His coming. Then comes the end, when He delivers the kingdom to God the Father, when He puts an end to all rule and all authority and power. For He must reign till He has put all enemies under His feet. The last enemy that will be destroyed is death. For "He has put all things under His feet." But when He says "all things are put under Him," it is evident that He who put all things under Him is excepted. Now when all things are made subject to Him, then the Son Himself will also be subject to Him who put all things under Him, that God may be all in all." 1 Corinthians 15:20-23

"He is the image of the invisible God, the firstborn over all creation. For by Him all things were created that are in heaven and that are on earth, visible and invisible, whether thrones or dominions or principalities or powers. All things were created through Him and for Him. And He is before all things, and in Him all things consist. And He is the head of the body, the church, who is the beginning, the firstborn from the dead, that in all things He may have the preeminence. For it pleased the Father that in Him all the fullness should dwell, and by Him to reconcile all things to Himself, by Him, whether things on earth or things in heaven, having made peace through the blood of His cross." Colossians 1:15-20

"John, to the seven churches which are in Asia: Grace to you and peace from Him who is and who was and who is to come, and from the seven Spirits who are before His throne, and from Jesus Christ, the faithful witness, the firstborn from the dead, and the ruler over the kings of the earth. To Him who loved us and washed us from our sins in His own blood, and has made us kings and priests to His God and Father, to Him be glory and dominion forever and ever. Amen."
Revelation 1:4-6

Celebrating The Spring Feasts
Book Suggestions

Celebrating Passover in the context of a Seder is one of the most deeply profound ways to introduce your family to the Biblical feasts. If your church does not celebrate Passover in the context of a Seder consider having your own at home with your family. You may even decide to include other believers in Jesus that are interested in learning about and celebrating the Biblical feasts with you. My favorite Passover Haggadah to recommend for use comes from the ministry "One for Israel". You can access this resource at: oneforisrael.org/passover-download/ or email me at elementalfaithpublishing@gmail.com to request a PDF copy.

In the weeks leading up to Passover you can begin to prepare your family by reading books and storybook Bibles together in addition to the Biblical text itself. Here are some recommendations:

Ages 0+
- Passover is Coming (Board book) — By: Tracy Newman
- My First Passover (Board book) — By: Tomie dePaola
- What Do You See? On Pesach (Board book) — By: Bracha Goetz
- Holy Week: An Emotions Primer (Board book) — By: Danielle Hitchen
- The Garden, The Curtain and the Cross (Board Book) — By: Carl Laferton

Ages 3+
- The Story of Passover (Board book) — By: Rabbi Francis Barry Silberg
- The Spring Feasts — By: Jessica AcMoody
- Jesus Calling: The Story of Easter — By: Sarah Young
- Jesus Rose for Me: The True Story of Easter — By: Jared Kennedy

Ages 5+
- The Garden, The Curtain and the Cross — By: Carl Laferton
- The Story of Passover — By: David A. Adler

Storybook Bible Suggestions

These are my favorite storybook Bibles to use with kids:
Jesus Calling Bible Storybook by Sarah Young is great for ages 3 and up. The are few enough words per page to hold a toddler's attention, but the stories themselves and illustrations are so well done that kids of all ages above 3 years old would enjoy this Bible. The Jesus Storybook Bible by Sally Lloyd- Jones is great for ages 5 and up. There are more words per page and slightly more complex stories, the stories themselves and illustrations are so well done that kids of all ages above 5 years old would enjoy this Bible. The Action Bible by Sergio Cariello is great for ages 8 and up. The text is more complex and definitely deeper, more mature content matter. This is a bit harder to use as a read-aloud as the Bible reads in a comic book style and following the pictures with the words is important to fully appreciate the whole story.

Below is a breakdown of relevant stories in each of these storybook Bibles that you could read with your children (age relevant) as you prepare to celebrate the Spring Feasts.

Jesus Calling Bible Storybook
By: Sarah Young
- The Story of Moses: The Passover (p.66-67)
- The Story of Moses: Moses the Great Leader (p.68-71)
- Palm Sunday (p.204-205) & The Last Supper (p.206-209)
- Jesus is Arrested (p.210-211) & Peter Denies Jesus (p.212-213)
- Good Friday (p.214-219) & Easter Sunday (p.220-223)

The Jesus Storybook Bible
By: Sally Lloyd-Jones
- God to the Rescue! (p.84-91) & God Makes A Way (p.92-99)
- The Servant King (p.286-293) & A Dark Night in the Garden (p.294-301)
- The Sun Stops Shining (p.302-309) & God's Wonderful Surprise (p.310-318)

The Action Bible
By: Sergio Cariello
- Spokesmen for God (p.133-136) & The Plagues (p.137-142)
- The FInal Plague (143-146) & 20,000 Egyptians Under the Sea (p.147-154)
- Palm Sunday (p.676-678) & Passover Problems (p.687-690)
- The Lord's Supper (p.691-694) & Crucified! (p.703-708)
- The Sealed Tomb (p.709-712)

Activities

Act Out the Passover Story

*Note: This activity will get a bit messy. I recommend setting up a space outdoors to act out the Exodus story with your family so you don't have to worry about the mess in your house.

Supplies needed:
- Bowl of water and red food coloring (plague of blood)
- Toy or paper frogs (plague of frogs)
- Small bowl full of sand (plague of lice)
- Hole puncher and black construction paper (plague of flies)
- Toy farm animals (plague against livestock)
- Red dot stickers (plague of boils)
- Ice cubes (plague of hail)
- Wooden clothespins (plague of locusts)
- Roll of craft paper, paintbrush and red paint (blood on the doorpost)

Decide who will play the various roles in the Exodus story: Narrator, Pharaoh, Moses, Egyptians, and Israelites. Make sure the narrator is an adult or a very strong reader. The narrator will read the scripture quoted below as everyone acts out the story:

"Afterward Moses and Aaron went in and told Pharaoh, "Thus says the Lord God of Israel: 'Let My people go, that they may hold a feast to Me in the wilderness.' "And Pharaoh said, "Who is the Lord, that I should obey His voice to let Israel go? I do not know the Lord, nor will I let Israel go." So they said, "The God of the Hebrews has met with us. Please, let us go three days' journey into the desert and sacrifice to the Lord our God, lest He fall upon us with pestilence or with the sword."" Exodus 5:1-3

"Then the Lord said to Moses, "Now you shall see what I will do to Pharaoh. For with a strong hand he will let them go, and with a strong hand he will drive them out of his land."" Exodus 6:1

"So the Lord said to Moses: "Pharaoh's heart is hard; he refuses to let the people go. Go to Pharaoh in the morning, when he goes out to the water, and you shall stand by the river's bank to meet him; and the rod which was turned to a serpent you shall take in your hand. And you shall say to him, 'The Lord God of the Hebrews has sent me to you, saying, "Let My people go, that they may serve Me in the wilderness"; but indeed, until now you would not hear!

Thus says the Lord: "By this you shall know that I am the Lord. Behold, I will strike the waters which are in the river with the rod that is in my hand, and they shall be turned to blood. And the fish that are in the river shall die, the river shall stink, and the Egyptians will loathe to drink the water of the river." '" Exodus 7:14-18

"And Moses and Aaron did so, just as the Lord commanded. So he lifted up the rod and struck the waters that were in the river, in the sight of Pharaoh and in the sight of his servants. And all the waters that were in the river were turned to blood." Exodus 7:20

"And the Lord spoke to Moses, "Go to Pharaoh and say to him, 'Thus says the Lord: "Let My people go, that they may serve Me. But if you refuse to let them go, behold, I will smite all your territory with frogs." Exodus 8:1-2

"Then the Lord spoke to Moses, "Say to Aaron, 'Stretch out your hand with your rod over the streams, over the rivers, and over the ponds, and cause frogs to come up on the land of Egypt.' " So Aaron stretched out his hand over the waters of Egypt, and the frogs came up and covered the land of Egypt." Exodus 8:5-6

Then Pharaoh called for Moses and Aaron, and said, "Entreat the Lord that He may take away the frogs from me and from my people; and I will let the people go, that they may sacrifice to the Lord." Exodus 8:8

"But when Pharaoh saw that there was relief, he hardened his heart and did not heed them, as the Lord had said." Exodus 8:15

"So the Lord said to Moses, "Say to Aaron, 'Stretch out your rod, and strike the dust of the land, so that it may become lice throughout all the land of Egypt.' "" Exodus 8:16

"But Pharaoh's heart grew hard, and he did not heed them, just as the Lord had said." Exodus 8:19b

"And the Lord said to Moses, "Rise early in the morning and stand before Pharaoh as he comes out to the water. Then say to him, 'Thus says the Lord: "Let My people go, that they may serve Me. Or else, if you will not let My people go, behold, I will send swarms of flies on you and your servants, on your people and into your houses. The houses of the Egyptians shall be full of swarms of flies, and also the ground on which they stand." Exodus 8:20-21

So Pharaoh said, "I will let you go, that you may sacrifice to the Lord your God in the wilderness; only you shall not go very far away. Intercede for me." Exodus 8:28

"So Moses went out from Pharaoh and entreated the Lord. And the Lord did according to the word of Moses; He removed the swarms of flies from Pharaoh, from his servants, and from his people. Not one remained. But Pharaoh hardened his heart at this time also; neither would he let the people go." Exodus 8:30-32

"Then the Lord said to Moses, "Go in to Pharaoh and tell him, 'Thus says the Lord God of the Hebrews: "Let My people go, that they may serve Me. For if you refuse to let them go, and still hold them, behold, the hand of the Lord will be on your cattle in the field, on the horses, on the donkeys, on the camels, on the oxen, and on the sheep—a very severe pestilence. And the Lord will make a difference between the livestock of Israel and the livestock of Egypt. So nothing shall die of all that belongs to the children of Israel." ' " Then the Lord appointed a set time, saying, "Tomorrow the Lord will do this thing in the land."

So the Lord did this thing on the next day, and all the livestock of Egypt died; but of the livestock of the children of Israel, not one died. Then Pharaoh sent, and indeed, not even one of the livestock of the Israelites was dead. But the heart of Pharaoh became hard, and he did not let the people go." Exodus 9:1-7

"So the Lord said to Moses and Aaron, "Take for yourselves handfuls of ashes from a furnace, and let Moses scatter it toward the heavens in the sight of Pharaoh. And it will become fine dust in all the land of Egypt, and it will cause boils that break out in sores on man and beast throughout all the land of Egypt." Then they took ashes from the furnace and stood before Pharaoh, and Moses scattered them toward heaven. And they caused boils that break out in sores on man and beast. 11 And the magicians could not stand before Moses because of the boils, for the boils were on the magicians and on all the Egyptians. But the Lord hardened the heart of Pharaoh; and he did not heed them, just as the Lord had spoken to Moses." Exodus 9:8-12

"Then the Lord said to Moses, "Rise early in the morning and stand before Pharaoh, and say to him, 'Thus says the Lord God of the Hebrews: "Let My people go, that they may serve Me, for at this time I will send all My plagues to your very heart, and on your servants and on your people, that you may know that there is none like Me in all the earth. Now if I had stretched out My hand and struck you and your people with pestilence, then you would have been cut off from the earth. But indeed for this purpose I have raised you up, that I may show My power in you, and that My name may be declared in all the earth. As yet you exalt yourself against My people in that you will not let them go. Behold, tomorrow about this time I will cause very heavy hail to rain down, such as has not been in Egypt since its founding until now. Therefore send now and gather your livestock and all that you have in the field, for the hail shall come down on every man and every animal which is found in the field and is not brought home; and they shall die." '" Exodus 9:13-19

"And Pharaoh sent and called for Moses and Aaron, and said to them, "I have sinned this time. The Lord is righteous, and my people and I are wicked. Entreat the Lord, that there may be no more mighty thundering and hail, for it is enough. I will let you go, and you shall stay no longer.""
Exodus 9:27-28

"And when Pharaoh saw that the rain, the hail, and the thunder had ceased, he sinned yet more; and he hardened his heart, he and his servants. So the heart of Pharaoh was hard; neither would he let the children of Israel go, as the Lord had spoken by Moses." Exodus 9:34-35

"So Moses and Aaron came in to Pharaoh and said to him, "Thus says the Lord God of the Hebrews: 'How long will you refuse to humble yourself before Me? Let My people go, that they may serve Me. Or else, if you refuse to let My people go, behold, tomorrow I will bring locusts into your territory." Exodus 10:3-4

"Then Pharaoh called for Moses and Aaron in haste, and said, "I have sinned against the Lord your God and against you. Now therefore, please forgive my sin only this once, and entreat the Lord your God, that He may take away from me this death only."" Exodus 10:16-17

"But the Lord hardened Pharaoh's heart, and he did not let the children of Israel go." Exodus 10:20

"Then the Lord said to Moses, "Stretch out your hand toward heaven, that there may be darkness over the land of Egypt, darkness which may even be felt."" Exodus 10:21

"Then Pharaoh called to Moses and said, "Go, serve the Lord; only let your flocks and your herds be kept back. Let your little ones also go with you."" Exodus 10:24

"But the Lord hardened Pharaoh's heart, and he would not let them go." Exodus 10:27

"And the Lord said to Moses, "I will bring one more plague on Pharaoh and on Egypt. Afterward he will let you go from here. When he lets you go, he will surely drive you out of here altogether." Exodus 11:1

"Then Moses said, "Thus says the Lord: 'About midnight I will go out into the midst of Egypt; and all the firstborn in the land of Egypt shall die, from the firstborn of Pharaoh who sits on his throne, even to the firstborn of the female servant who is behind the handmill, and all the firstborn of the animals." Exodus 11:4-5

"But the Lord said to Moses, "Pharaoh will not heed you, so that My wonders may be multiplied in the land of Egypt." So Moses and Aaron did all these wonders before Pharaoh; and the Lord hardened Pharaoh's heart, and he did not let the children of Israel go out of his land." Exodus 11:9-10

"And they shall take some of the blood and put it on the two doorposts and on the lintel of the houses where they eat it." Exodus 12:7

"'For I will pass through the land of Egypt on that night, and will strike all the firstborn in the land of Egypt, both man and beast; and against all the gods of Egypt I will execute judgment: I am the Lord. Now the blood shall be a sign for you on the houses where you are. And when I see the blood, I will pass over you; and the plague shall not be on you to destroy you when I strike the land of Egypt." Exodus 12:12-13

"And it came to pass at midnight that the Lord struck all the firstborn in the land of Egypt, from the firstborn of Pharaoh who sat on his throne to the firstborn of the captive who was in the dungeon, and all the firstborn of livestock." Then he called for Moses and Aaron by night, and said, "Rise, go out from among my people, both you and the children of Israel. And go, serve the Lord as you have said. Also take your flocks and your herds, as you have said, and be gone; and bless me also." Exodus 12:29 & 31-32

Clean the House

Part of preparing for Passover is cleaning the house; think spring cleaning! Take some time as a family and divide up jobs, everyone gets to work on something. Washing windows, mopping floors, deep cleaning the things that have gone neglected for months (that would be washing windows for me!) Tell your kids there will be a game and snack once everyone finishes their assigned jobs. Then see the next activity for inspiration.

Search Your Home for Leaven - Snack time!

In the Bible God's people were told to remove all the leaven from their homes; leaven being a symbol of sin. Have your kids go through your pantry/fridge and see if they can find all of the foods containing leaven (yeast). Then have a quick snack as you read or recall the story of God's people removing all the leaven from their homes. You can find the story in your favorite Storybook Bible or a full Bible (Exodus 12:14-20).

Bake Bread Leavened and Unleavened

Baking bread both leavened and unleavened will help your child understand the role of yeast in bread; how it helps "puff it up". Bread making may be something you do on a regular basis with your family or maybe like my family this would be a new endeavor. There are tons of great recipes you can find for leavened and unleavened bread with a quick internet search.

After you have baked your bread and have spent sometime observing and comparing the two different types of bread have a conversation with your child about how the Bible compares leaven to sin. Spend some time together praying, reflecting and asking Jesus to show you sin in your hearts. This would be a wonderful time to share your personal testimony with your child of how Jesus has changed your life and leads you daily in repentance. Consider the age of your child and be sure to adjust content and language for their comprehension.

Decorate an Elijah Cup

Part of the Seder meal is setting out a cup for Elijah at the table. You can have some fun with this part of the Seder prior to your meal and decorate the cup that you will set out for Elijah. A plastic wine cup can be drawn on with permanent markers; ribbons, jewels, etc can be glued on. Or you may opt for a paper cup that can be drawn on with crayons or washable markers. Whatever supplies you choose, have fun decorating as you eagerly prepare for the Passover Seder.

Communion and Foot Washing

Grab your favorite Storybook Bible or a full Bible (depending on the age of your children) and read the story of the Last Supper (Matthew 26:17-30 or Mark 14:12-26 or Luke 22:7-20) and Jesus washing the disciple's feet in John 13:1-17. Remember that the context of the Last Supper was a Passover Seder which you may be doing at your church or choose to do as a family at home. This activity will be a much shorter version and more like the style of communion most Western churches have.

Read aloud the story of the Last Supper, give time for your children to comment on anything that stood out to them. Take some time to marvel at Jesus' sacrifice for our sin so we could be one with the Father forever. Share with your children how the word of God says we are not to partake of the bread and the drink in an "unworthy manner." Spend a few minutes as a family confessing anything God brings to your heart that needs repenting. As the parent lead the way in this, it could be as simple as confessing to your children how you spoke to them that day was a sin and taking the time to ask their forgiveness if you haven't yet done that. Don't press the issue if your children don't say anything even though you know they hit their sibling that day, lied, etc and still have not apologized. Take the route of being an example of what repentance looks like and silently pray that the Lord would work in their hearts. Forced apologies and forgiveness isn't true forgiveness. *Note: make the judgment call to skip over this activity if your child is too young for this concept and communion. Maybe they are having a rough day and not in the right mindset for something as sacred as communion.

Break bread together and remember Jesus' words "This is my body, which is given for you. Do this in remembrance of me." Then share the juice together remembering Jesus' words "This cup is the New Covenant between God and his people - an agreement confirmed with my blood, which is poured out as a sacrifice for you."

After sharing the bread and the juice together read the story of Jesus washing the disciple's feet. Have a large bowl of water and some towels available and spend time washing each others feet. You may choose to have each person say a blessing over the person whose feet they are washing.

Make a Seder Plate

A Seder plate is used in the context of a Passover Seder which you may be doing at your church or at home with your family. However, it's also fun to let your kids explore the Seder plate a bit. Head back to the section where the Seder elements are discussed to refresh your memory of what goes on the seder plate. Then have fun snacking and recounting God's faithfulness to His people through each of the elements. If you have younger kids you could do a quick overview of what each of the elements are and represent. If you have older kids you could have them pull out their Bibles and do a quick hunt through Scripture taking turns reading passages that relate to each of the elements as they snack.

Afikomen Hide and Seek

Part of the Seder meal is hunting for the afikomen, you can read more about the meaning of the afikomen back in the Seder elements section of this teaching guide. This is great as a stand alone activity in addition to it's part in the Seder meal. Give your kids a quick explanation of what the afikomen represents. The broken matzah represents Jesus body broken for us. Wrapping the matzah represents Jesus buried in the grave. Finding the hidden matzah represents Jesus resurrecting from the grave. Take turns wrapping up a piece of broken matzah in a cloth and hiding it around the house. Have fun with this afikomen hide and seek!

Build a Lego Pyramid & Make your Own Bricks

The Passover story is one of freedom; God leading His people out of slavery in Egypt. To commemorate the Israelites' time in bondage making bricks, you can have your children make their own bricks and build. Grab a handful of yellow legos and build your own pyramids. Or make your own bricks using "moon sand" and ice cube trays. Moon sand can be made by mixing 1/4 a cup of baby oil for every 2 cups of flour. Pack the mixture into ice cube trays and then build with the cubes that you've created.

Feast of Weeks

To celebrate another of God's holy feasts, we count 50 days from First Fruits till Feast of Weeks.

This feast of the Lord is a time of thanksgiving, celebrating summer harvests that sustain people's living.

During this time God gave Israel the Torah, His law full of promises, provision the people experienced and saw.

To honor the Lord, freewill offerings people gave,
to remember God's goodness and how He came to save.

During the time of harvest at this special feast,
gleanings were left in the field for both poor man and beast.

These gleanings that were left are a picture of God's heart,
to unite Jew and Gentile, forming a special family set apart.

Ruth 4:21-22 Ruth married Boaz at this special time,
their union points to Jesus who came from this family line.

During the Feast of Weeks two loaves of bread are given,
as an offering, a union between Jew and Gentile with the God of Heaven.

After Jesus was resurrected He told His disciples to go,
to the upper room to wait for His promised power to show.

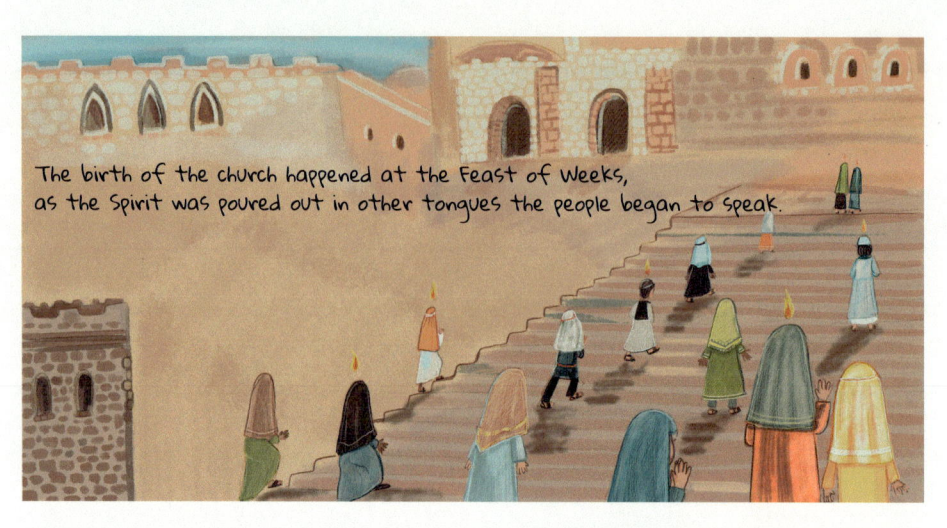

The birth of the church happened at the Feast of Weeks,
as the Spirit was poured out in other tongues the people began to speak.

This baptism of fire gave zeal to the new church,
to boldly teach about Jesus in hearts the Spirit would search.

This outpouring of the Spirit we call Pentecost,
the helper sent from Heaven to seek and save the lost.

What is the Feast of Weeks?

The Feast of Weeks takes place 50 days after Passover and is a festival celebrating the end of the barley harvest and the first fruits of the wheat harvest. The word "pente" means 50, a reference to the counting of the harvest 50 days after Passover. The Hebrew name Shavout means "weeks". At the Feast of Weeks, we recount God giving His people, Israel, the Torah, at Mount Sinai. Jesus came as the fulfillment of the law and then ascended to Heaven.

Jesus told His disciples to go and wait for the helper from heaven to come after His ascension to heaven. The Holy Spirit was poured so that God's law could be written on human hearts through relationship with Jesus. Let's go on a journey through Scripture and recall these amazing events! We'll begin in Leviticus 23:15-22 where God gives instructions for the Feast of Weeks:

"'And you shall count for yourselves from the day after the Sabbath, from the day that you brought the sheaf of the wave offering: seven Sabbaths shall be completed. Count fifty days to the day after the seventh Sabbath; then you shall offer a new grain offering to the Lord. You shall bring from your dwellings two wave loaves of two-tenths of an ephah. They shall be of fine flour; they shall be baked with leaven. They are the firstfruits to the Lord. And you shall offer with the bread seven lambs of the first year, without blemish, one young bull, and two rams. They shall be as a burnt offering to the Lord, with their grain offering and their drink offerings, an offering made by fire for a sweet aroma to the Lord. Then you shall sacrifice one kid of the goats as a sin offering, and two male lambs of the first year as a sacrifice of a peace offering. The priest shall wave them with the bread of the first-fruits as a wave offering before the Lord, with the two lambs. They shall be holy to the Lord for the priest. And you shall proclaim on the same day that it is a holy convocation to you. You shall do no customary work on it. It shall be a statute forever in all your dwellings throughout your generations.

'When you reap the harvest of your land, you shall not wholly reap the corners of your field when you reap, nor shall you gather any gleaning from your harvest. You shall leave them for the poor and for the stranger: I am the Lord your God.' "

Following tradition on the first day of Passover farmers went out to survey their harvest, looking for the buds that sprang up first; special ribbons would mark those buds. Over the next 50 days the farmers would tend to their crops as usual but giving special attention to those that were marked. On the 50th day all the plants marked were to be cut and the entire crop of "first fruits" brought to the Temple.

For the sake of brevity I am not including the entire text of the giving of the law in this teaching guide. However, I would highly recommend that you take some time to reacquaint yourself with these chapters in Exodus. Read or listen to Exodus 19-24 & 31-35 before reading further through this section of the teaching guide.

Now jump to the New Testament and recall Jesus' instructions to His disciples right before He ascended to heaven, let's read Acts 1:1-14 and Acts 2:

"The former account I made, O Theophilus, of all that Jesus began both to do and teach, until the day in which He was taken up, after He through the Holy Spirit had given commandments to the apostles whom He had chosen, to whom He also presented Himself alive after His suffering by many infallible proofs, being seen by them during forty days and speaking of the things pertaining to the kingdom of God.

And being assembled together with them, He commanded them not to depart from Jerusalem, but to wait for the Promise of the Father, "which," He said, "you have heard from Me; for John truly baptized with water, but you shall be baptized with the Holy Spirit not many days from now." Therefore, when they had come together, they asked Him, saying, "Lord, will You at this time restore the kingdom to Israel?" And He said to them, "It is not for you to know times or seasons which the Father has put in His own authority. But you shall receive power when the Holy Spirit has come upon you; and you shall be witnesses to Me in Jerusalem, and in all Judea and Samaria, and to the end of the earth."

Now when He had spoken these things, while they watched, He was taken up, and a cloud received Him out of their sight. And while they looked steadfastly toward heaven as He went up, behold, two men stood by them in white apparel, who also said, "Men of Galilee, why do you stand gazing up into heaven? This same Jesus, who was taken up from you into heaven, will so come in like manner as you saw Him go into heaven."

Then they returned to Jerusalem from the mount called Olivet, which is near Jerusalem, a Sabbath day's journey. And when they had entered, they went up into the upper room where they were staying: Peter, James, John, and Andrew; Philip and Thomas; Bartholomew and Matthew; James the son of Alphaeus and Simon the Zealot; and Judas the son of James. These all continued with one accord in prayer and supplication, with the women and Mary the mother of Jesus, and with His brothers."

Acts 2

When the Day of Pentecost had fully come, they were all with one accord in one place. And suddenly there came a sound from heaven, as of a rushing mighty wind, and it filled the whole house where they were sitting. Then there appeared to them divided tongues, as of fire, and one sat upon each of them. And they were all filled with the Holy Spirit and began to speak with other tongues, as the Spirit gave them utterance.

And there were dwelling in Jerusalem Jews, devout men, from every nation under heaven. And when this sound occurred, the multitude came together, and were confused, because everyone heard them speak in his own language. Then they were all amazed and marveled, saying to one another, "Look, are not all these who speak Galileans? And how is it that we hear, each in our own language in which we were born? Parthians and Medes and Elamites, those dwelling in Mesopotamia, Judea and Cappadocia, Pontus and Asia, Phrygia and Pamphylia, Egypt and the parts of Libya adjoining Cyrene, visitors from Rome, both Jews and proselytes, Cretans and Arabs—we hear them speaking in our own tongues the wonderful works of God." So they were all amazed and perplexed, saying to one another, "Whatever could this mean?"

Others mocking said, "They are full of new wine."

But Peter, standing up with the eleven, raised his voice and said to them, "Men of Judea and all who dwell in Jerusalem, let this be known to you, and heed my words. For these are not drunk, as you suppose, since it is only the third hour of the day. But this is what was spoken by the prophet Joel:

'And it shall come to pass in the last days, says God,
That I will pour out of My Spirit on all flesh;
Your sons and your daughters shall prophesy,
Your young men shall see visions,
Your old men shall dream dreams.
And on My menservants and on My maidservants
I will pour out My Spirit in those days;
And they shall prophesy.
I will show wonders in heaven above
And signs in the earth beneath:
Blood and fire and vapor of smoke.

The sun shall be turned into darkness,
And the moon into blood,
Before the coming of the great and awesome day of the Lord.
And it shall come to pass
That whoever calls on the name of the Lord
Shall be saved.'

"Men of Israel, hear these words: Jesus of Nazareth, a Man attested by God to you by miracles, wonders, and signs which God did through Him in your midst, as you yourselves also know— Him, being delivered by the determined purpose and foreknowledge of God, you have taken by lawless hands, have crucified, and put to death; whom God raised up, having loosed the pains of death, because it was not possible that He should be held by it. For David says concerning Him:

'I foresaw the Lord always before my face,
For He is at my right hand, that I may not be shaken.
Therefore my heart rejoiced, and my tongue was glad;
Moreover my flesh also will rest in hope.
For You will not leave my soul in Hades,
Nor will You allow Your Holy One to see corruption.
You have made known to me the ways of life;
You will make me full of joy in Your presence.'

"Men and brethren, let me speak freely to you of the patriarch David, that he is both dead and buried, and his tomb is with us to this day. Therefore, being a prophet, and knowing that God had sworn with an oath to him that of the fruit of his body, according to the flesh, He would raise up the Christ to sit on his throne, he, foreseeing this, spoke concerning the resurrection of the Christ, that His soul was not left in Hades, nor did His flesh see corruption. This Jesus God has raised up, of which we are all witnesses. Therefore being exalted to the right hand of God, and having received from the Father the promise of the Holy Spirit, He poured out this which you now see and hear.

"For David did not ascend into the heavens, but he says himself:
'The Lord said to my Lord, "Sit at My right hand, Till I make Your enemies Your footstool." '

"Therefore let all the house of Israel know assuredly that God has made this Jesus, whom you crucified, both Lord and Christ."

Now when they heard this, they were cut to the heart, and said to Peter and the rest of the apostles, "Men and brethren, what shall we do?"

Then Peter said to them, "Repent, and let every one of you be baptized in the name of Jesus Christ for the remission of sins; and you shall receive the gift of the Holy Spirit. For the promise is to you and to your children, and to all who are afar off, as many as the Lord our God will call."

And with many other words he testified and exhorted them, saying, "Be saved from this perverse generation." Then those who gladly received his word were baptized; and that day about three thousand souls were added to them. And they continued steadfastly in the apostles' doctrine and fellowship, in the breaking of bread, and in prayers. Then fear came upon every soul, and many wonders and signs were done through the apostles. Now all who believed were together, and had all things in common, and sold their possessions and goods, and divided them among all, as anyone had need.

So continuing daily with one accord in the temple, and breaking bread from house to house, they ate their food with gladness and simplicity of heart, praising God and having favor with all the people. And the Lord added to the church daily those who were being saved.

It's this moment of time in Acts 2 where we see the birth of the Church occur. We see God making a way, by His Spirit, for all Gentiles who would come to the knowledge of Jesus to be a part of His family. Jesus came as the fulfillment to the law and the coming of the Holy Spirit meant that the law could be written on human hearts. Praise God that we have a helper so that we might live holy, righteous, and set apart, not by works of our own hands but by the grace of the Spirit.

"Therefore, brethren, we are debtors—not to the flesh, to live according to the flesh. For if you live according to the flesh you will die; but if by the Spirit you put to death the deeds of the body, you will live. For as many as are led by the Spirit of God, these are sons of God. For you did not receive the spirit of bondage again to fear, but you received the Spirit of adoption by whom we cry out, "Abba, Father." The Spirit Himself bears witness with our spirit that we are children of God, and if children, then heirs—heirs of God and joint heirs with Christ, if indeed we suffer with Him, that we may also be glorified together." Romans 8:12-17

The Feast of Weeks is a time for celebrating God giving His law to the Israelites and the coming of the Holy Spirit so that God's law could be written on our hearts. Jesus by His Spirit invites us into His family forever, a beautiful union of Jew and Gentile. Consider Paul's words to the Galatians regarding the law and Christ:

"What purpose then does the law serve? It was added because of transgressions, till the Seed should come to whom the promise was made; and it was appointed through angels by the hand of a mediator. Now a mediator does not mediate for one only, but God is one.

Is the law then against the promises of God? Certainly not! For if there had been a law given which could have given life, truly righteousness would have been by the law. But the Scripture has confined all under sin, that the promise by faith in Jesus Christ might be given to those who believe. But before faith came, we were kept under guard by the law, kept for the faith which would afterward be revealed. Therefore the law was our tutor to bring us to Christ, that we might be justified by faith. But after faith has come, we are no longer under a tutor.

For you are all sons of God through faith in Christ Jesus. For as many of you as were baptized into Christ have put on Christ. There is neither Jew nor Greek, there is neither slave nor free, there is neither male nor female; for you are all one in Christ Jesus. And if you are Christ's, then you are Abraham's seed, and heirs according to the promise." Galatians 3:19-29

Between the Exodus story and the birth of the church in Acts is another story set at the time of the barley harvest (during the Feast of Weeks): the book of Ruth. There is some really powerful symbolism that God institutes in the Leviticus 23 instructions regarding the two loaves of bread waved before the Lord; they are a symbol of Jew and Gentile. Note the text of Leviticus 23:22 where God instructs His people to leave gleanings in the field from the harvest then take a few minutes and read or listen through the book of Ruth in it's entirety.

The book of Ruth is a beautiful story of redemption, Boaz the kinsman redeemer an archetype of Jesus. Did you know that the union between Ruth and Boaz brought about the lineage of King David from whom Jesus descended? See Ruth 4:18-22. The gleanings which God commanded to be left in the field were a picture of God's heart to bring both Jew and Gentile together. Ruth, a Moabite, marries Boaz, an Israelite, and their union brings about the line from which the Messiah would descend. We'll close this section on the history of the Feast of Weeks with Romans 11:11-18. As you read this passage consider how you might pray for and be a witness to Jewish people.

"I say then, have they stumbled that they should fall? Certainly not! But through their fall, to provoke them to jealousy, salvation has come to the Gentiles. Now if their fall is riches for the world, and their failure riches for the Gentiles, how much more their fullness!

For I speak to you Gentiles; inasmuch as I am an apostle to the Gentiles, I magnify my ministry, if by any means I may provoke to jealousy those who are my flesh and save some of them. For if their being cast away is the reconciling of the world, what will their acceptance be but life from the dead?

For if the firstfruit is holy, the lump is also holy; and if the root is holy, so are the branches. And if some of the branches were broken off, and you, being a wild olive tree, were grafted in among them, and with them became a partaker of the root and fatness of the olive tree, do not boast against the branches. But if you do boast, remember that you do not support the root, but the root supports you." Romans 11:11-18

Celebrating the Feast of Weeks
Book Suggestions

Ages 0+
- What Do You See? On ShavuosBy: Bracha Goetz
- The Holy Spirit (Board Book)By: Devon Provencher

Ages 3+
- The Feast of WeeksBy: Jessica AcMoody
- Jesus Calling Bible StorybookBy: Sarah Young
    - The Ten Commandments (p.72-34)
    - Ruth and Naomi (p.88-89)
    - Jesus Goes to Heaven (p.226-227)
    - Joy Came Down (p.228-231)

Ages 5+
- The Jesus Storybook BibleBy: Sally Lloyd-Jones
    - Ten Ways to Be Perfect (p.100-107)
    - Going Home (p.318-325)
    - God Sends Help (p.326-333)

Ages 8+
- The Action BibleBy: Sergio Cariello
    - Good Advice (p.163-164)
    - God's Commandments (p.165)
    - Ruth's Redeemer (p.254-259)
    - Seeing Jesus Again (p.713-718)
    - Waiting for the Spirit (p.719-721)
    - Tongues of Fire (p.722-726)

Activities

Counting the Omer

The counting of the omer refers to the 50 day period between Passover and the Feast of Weeks. God commands His people to count 50 days until the beginning of the harvest season, see Leviticus 23:15-22. As Passover ends you and your family can begin looking forward to God's next appointed feast with excitement, by counting the days. With your family incorporate counting the omer into your dinner time routine. Begin counting the omer the night following Passover. After finishing dinner, before leaving the table, have one family member recite the blessing over each day:

"Blessed are you, Adonai our God, Sovereign of the Universe, who has sanctified us with your commandments and commanded us to count the omer."

Then after the blessing recite the appropriate day for the count:

"Today is the first day of the omer."

After the first six days it is traditional to also include the number of weeks that are counted:

"Today is 10 days, which is one week and three days of the omer."

Create 10 Commandment Tablets

Grab some chart paper or a roll of craft paper as well as scissors and markers. Draw out two large tablets and write out the ten commandments on them. Cut out the tablets and hang them somewhere that you family can see them. Commit to praying daily that God would help you and your kids walk in God's ways according to His commandments. Pray that each person in your family would grow with a desire to hear and obey God's Word.

Dance with the Bible

The Feast of Weeks commemorates the giving of the law; an entrance into deeper relationship between God and His people. This is a joyful event and should be celebrated as such. So, grab your Bible, turn on some of your favorite worship music, and have a dance party as a family. Celebrate God giving His law to Israel and in turn to us through Jesus. Celebrate that God's Word can be written on our hearts because of the coming of the Holy Spirit.

Eat Snacks with Dairy

Eating foods containing dairy is a common tradition used to celebrate the Feast of Weeks. The Promised Land that God brought His people into was a land flowing with milk and honey. Eating foods with dairy helps commemorate this special time. Have fun deciding what special things you might eat to celebrate and remember God's faithfulness to His people. Maybe you'll decide to have ice cream sundaes, cheesecake, a variety of cheese and crackers, or quiche; have fun being creative!

Bake Challah Bread

The Feast of Weeks is a celebration of the grain harvest, so what better way to commemorate this special time than baking a loaf of bread? A internet search will provide you a variety of different breads you could bake. A traditional Jewish bread that is eaten is challah bread and a gluten free version is one of my favorites.

Make a Birthday Cake - Happy Birthday to the Church!

As you learned during your reading of the teaching portion on this feast, Jesus fulfills the Feast of Weeks. By sending the Holy Spirit, the Word of God can be written on our hearts. Celebrate the birth of the Church by baking a birthday cake together as a family. Pick out your favorite type of cake and have fun rejoicing in the work of God among His people!

Experience the Wind

Scripture likens the coming of the Holy Spirit to a mighty rushing wind. Spend sometime outdoors with your kids experiencing the wind. Lay out a blanket and sit or lie still as you feel the wind move around you. Watch the tops of the trees to see how the wind moves them. Hang a wind chime on your front porch or back deck. Have fun flying a kite. Help your kids make the connection that the Holy Spirit is like the wind. We cannot see the wind just like we cannot see the Holy Spirit, but we can see the effects of the wind on things and feel it. We can feel the presence of God through the Holy Spirit and see His work in our lives.

Dove - Prayer Cards
The Holy Spirit is often likened to a dove, think about the passage in the Gospels where the Spirit descends upon Jesus like a dove, baptizing Him. The Holy Spirit is the one who leads us in intercession to bring our needs and the needs of others to the Lord. Search for an outline of a dove or draw your own. You can have your kids paint or color the doves and write out prayers on them. You could even write out the names of people that you want to be reminded to pray for daily.

Spend Time in Prayer
Teaching your kids how to cultivate a prayer life is essential to their relationship with God. If your family doesn't pray at meal times that is a great place to start. Prayers before bedtime are also a great way to incorporate more prayer into you day. If you homeschool consider how to incorporate a time of prayer into your day with your children, this could also be done on the weekend if you send your children to school daily. Teach your children about different ways to pray; the Lords prayer, praying scripture, silent prayer, petitions (bringing our needs to God), thanksgiving and praise, having a conversation with God and listening to Him. Praise God that we can be in intimate connection with Him because of His Holy Spirit!

Light Candles as you Read the Story of Pentecost
Grab your favorite storybook Bible or a regular Bible and read the story of Pentecost; Acts 2. To create ambiance and imagine what tongues of fire might have looked like turn off the lights and light some candles. Read by candlelight as you remember God sending the promised helper from heaven, the Holy Spirit.

Wear Red
Red is the color commonly associated with Pentecost in Church tradition. If you attend a church that follows a liturgical calendar you are likely used to seeing red on the altar or red worn by your pastor or priest. Pick out some red clothes for you and your family to wear to remember the coming of the Holy Spirit.

Feast of Trumpets

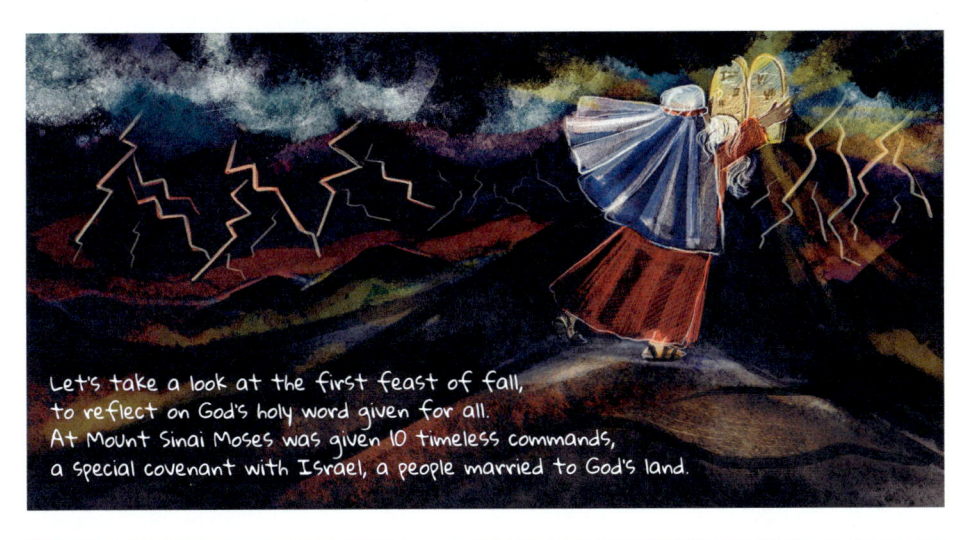

Let's take a look at the first feast of fall,
to reflect on God's holy word given for all.
At Mount Sinai Moses was given 10 timeless commands,
a special covenant with Israel, a people married to God's land.

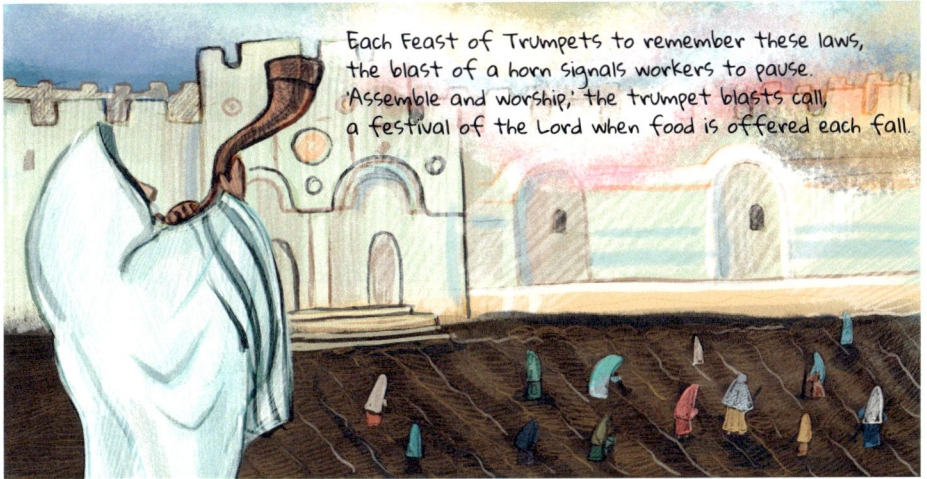

Each Feast of Trumpets to remember these laws,
the blast of a horn signals workers to pause.
'Assemble and worship,' the trumpet blasts call,
a festival of the Lord when food is offered each fall.

The seventh trumpet proclaims the final feast of this age,
Jesus returns, gathers His Bride, the world turns a new page.
The Kingdom of God on earth, here it will finally be,
with new bodies, like Jesus, the Bride adorned in white for all to see.

What is the Feast of Trumpets?

The Feast of Trumpets known as Rosh Hashanah occurs in the seventh month Tishri (usually in September). On the first day of the month, there is a memorial of blowing of trumpets. The trumpet blowing was a signal for the field workers to stop harvesting and leave immediately for worship at the Temple. Rosh Hashanah means "head of the year" and is the Jewish New Year.

"Then the LORD spoke to Moses, saying, "Speak to the children of Israel, saying: 'In the seventh month, on the first day of the month, you shall have a Sabbath-rest, a memorial of blowing of trumpets, a holy convocation. You shall do no customary work on it; and you shall offer an offering made by fire to the LORD.'" Leviticus 23:23-25

What is being commemorated or memorialized at the Feast of Trumpets? God's Covenant with His people Israel. Check out Exodus 19 & 20:

In the third month after the children of Israel had gone out of the land of Egypt, on the same day, they came to the Wilderness of Sinai. For they had departed from Rephidim, had come to the Wilderness of Sinai, and camped in the wilderness. So Israel camped there before the mountain.

And Moses went up to God, and the Lord called to him from the mountain, saying, "Thus you shall say to the house of Jacob, and tell the children of Israel: 'You have seen what I did to the Egyptians, and how I bore you on eagles' wings and brought you to Myself. Now therefore, if you will indeed obey My voice and keep My covenant, then you shall be a special treasure to Me above all people; for all the earth is Mine. And you shall be to Me a kingdom of priests and a holy nation.' These are the words which you shall speak to the children of Israel."

So Moses came and called for the elders of the people, and laid before them all these words which the Lord commanded him. Then all the people answered together and said, "All that the Lord has spoken we will do." So Moses brought back the words of the people to the Lord. And the Lord said to Moses, "Behold, I come to you in the thick cloud, that the people may hear when I speak with you, and believe you forever."

So Moses told the words of the people to the Lord.

Then the Lord said to Moses, "Go to the people and consecrate them today and tomorrow, and let them wash their clothes. And let them be ready for the third day. For on the third day the Lord will come down upon Mount Sinai in the sight of all the people. You shall set bounds for the people all around, saying, 'Take heed to yourselves that you do not go up to the mountain or touch its base. Whoever touches the mountain shall surely be put to death. Not a hand shall touch him, but he shall surely be stoned or shot with an arrow; whether man or beast, he shall not live.' When the trumpet sounds long, they shall come near the mountain."

So Moses went down from the mountain to the people and sanctified the people, and they washed their clothes. And he said to the people, "Be ready for the third day; do not come near your wives."

Then it came to pass on the third day, in the morning, that there were thunderings and lightnings, and a thick cloud on the mountain; and the sound of the trumpet was very loud, so that all the people who were in the camp trembled. And Moses brought the people out of the camp to meet with God, and they stood at the foot of the mountain. Now Mount Sinai was completely in smoke, because the Lord descended upon it in fire. Its smoke ascended like the smoke of a furnace, and the whole mountain quaked greatly. And when the blast of the trumpet sounded long and became louder and louder, Moses spoke, and God answered him by voice. Then the Lord came down upon Mount Sinai, on the top of the mountain. And the Lord called Moses to the top of the mountain, and Moses went up.

And the Lord said to Moses, "Go down and warn the people, lest they break through to gaze at the Lord, and many of them perish. Also let the priests who come near the Lord consecrate themselves, lest the Lord break out against them."

But Moses said to the Lord, "The people cannot come up to Mount Sinai; for You warned us, saying, 'Set bounds around the mountain and consecrate it.' "

Then the Lord said to him, "Away! Get down and then come up, you and Aaron with you. But do not let the priests and the people break through to come up to the Lord, lest He break out against them." So Moses went down to the people and spoke to them.

And God spoke all these words, saying:
"I am the Lord your God, who brought you out of the land of Egypt, out of the house of bondage.
"You shall have no other gods before Me.
"You shall not make for yourself a carved image—any likeness of anything that is in heaven above, or that is in the earth beneath, or that is in the water under the earth; you shall not bow down to them nor serve them. For I, the Lord your God, am a jealous God, visiting the iniquity of the fathers upon the children to the third and fourth generations of those who hate Me, but showing mercy to thousands, to those who love Me and keep My commandments.
"You shall not take the name of the Lord your God in vain, for the Lord will not hold him guiltless who takes His name in vain.
"Remember the Sabbath day, to keep it holy. Six days you shall labor and do all your work, but the seventh day is the Sabbath of the Lord your God. In it you shall do no work: you, nor your son, nor your daughter, nor your male servant, nor your female servant, nor your cattle, nor your stranger who is within your gates. For in six days the Lord made the heavens and the earth, the sea, and all that is in them, and rested the seventh day. Therefore the Lord blessed the Sabbath day and hallowed it.
"Honor your father and your mother, that your days may be long upon the land which the Lord your God is giving you.
"You shall not murder.
"You shall not commit adultery.
"You shall not steal.
"You shall not bear false witness against your neighbor.
"You shall not covet your neighbor's house; you shall not covet your neighbor's wife, nor his male servant, nor his female servant, nor his ox, nor his donkey, nor anything that is your neighbor's."

Now all the people witnessed the thunderings, the lightning flashes, the sound of the trumpet, and the mountain smoking; and when the people saw it, they trembled and stood afar off. Then they said to Moses, "You speak with us, and we will hear; but let not God speak with us, lest we die."

And Moses said to the people, "Do not fear; for God has come to test you, and that His fear may be before you, so that you may not sin." So the people stood afar off, but Moses drew near the thick darkness where God was.

Then the Lord said to Moses, "Thus you shall say to the children of Israel: 'You have seen that I have talked with you from heaven. You shall not make anything to be with Me—gods of silver or gods of gold you shall not make for yourselves. An altar of earth you shall make for Me, and you shall sacrifice on it your burnt offerings and your peace offerings, your sheep and your oxen. In every place where I record My name I will come to you, and I will bless you. And if you make Me an altar of stone, you shall not build it of hewn stone; for if you use your tool on it, you have profaned it. Nor shall you go up by steps to My altar, that your nakedness may not be exposed on it.'

God manifests His presence in smoke and fire on Mount Sinai as He came to covenant with His people amidst the sound of a trumpet that caused the people to tremble. The Israelites in turn promised to do everything the Lord commanded them to do. This event would be commemorated year after year by sounding trumpet blasts to remind Israel that they were a people under covenant; a nation who had committed to being God's people.

Why is this relevant to believers in Jesus? Did you know the final fulfillment of the Feast of Trumpets will occur when Jesus returns? Check out these passages to see what will happen:

"Immediately after the tribulation of those days the sun will be darkened, and the moon will not give its light; the stars will fall from heaven, and the powers of the heavens will be shaken. Then the sign of the Son of Man will appear in heaven, and then all the tribes of the earth will mourn, and they will see the Son of Man coming on the clouds of heaven with power and great glory. And He will send His angels with a great sound of a trumpet, and they will gather together His elect from the four winds, from one end of heaven to the other." Matthew 24:29-31

"But I do not want you to be ignorant, brethren, concerning those who have fallen asleep, lest you sorrow as others who have no hope. For if we believe that Jesus died and rose again, even so God will bring with Him those who sleep in Jesus.

For this we say to you by the word of the Lord, that we who are alive and remain until the coming of the Lord will by no means precede those who are asleep. For the Lord Himself will descend from heaven with a shout, with the voice of an archangel, and with the trumpet of God. And the dead in Christ will rise first. Then we who are alive and remain shall be caught up together with them in the clouds to meet the Lord in the air. And thus we shall always be with the Lord. Therefore comfort one another with these words." 1 Thessalonians 4:13-18

Now this I say, brethren, that flesh and blood cannot inherit the kingdom of God; nor does corruption inherit incorruption. Behold, I tell you a mystery: We shall not all sleep, but we shall all be changed." 1 Corinthians 15:50-51

"Then the seventh angel sounded: And there were loud voices in heaven, saying, "The kingdoms of this world have become the kingdoms of our Lord and of His Christ, and He shall reign forever and ever!" And the twenty-four elders who sat before God on their thrones fell on their faces and worshiped God, saying:

"We give You thanks, O Lord God Almighty,
The One who is and who was and who is to come,
Because You have taken Your great power and reigned.
The nations were angry, and Your wrath has come,
And the time of the dead, that they should be judged,
And that You should reward Your servants the prophets and the saints,
And those who fear Your name, small and great,
And should destroy those who destroy the earth."
Then the temple of God was opened in heaven, and the ark of His covenant was seen in His temple. And there were lightnings, noises, thunderings, an earthquake, and great hail." Revelation 11:15-19

The Feast of Trumpets will be fully fulfilled when Jesus appears in the sky at the 7th trumpet and Jesus "gathers" His Bride. This moment that is to come is our blessed hope as we will be transformed ready to join Jesus – we can long for this moment with hope and anticipation. Jesus will return at the Feast of Trumpets, the Bride will be gathered to meet Him in the air, receive new bodies, and the Kingdom of God of Earth will be inaugurated.

Day of Atonement

The first Day of Atonement happened a long time ago,
Moses ascended the mountain to bring God's commands back below.
Instead of waiting for Moses and the word of the Lord to come,
the Hebrews built a calf to worship, made of gold from Egypt, a hefty sum.

The idol worship from God's people made Him very mad,
the Lord told Moses He would destroy them for being bad.
But Moses pleaded and said to the Lord.
"Forgive all their sin, let your mercy be poured!"
God forgave the people and made atonement for their sin,
each year Israel remembers His kindness towards their kin.

Yearly on this day in the temple the priest would stand,
performing the sacrifice to cleanse the people and land.
The priest swapped His colorful robes for simple robes of white,
pointing to Jesus, who left the splendor of Heaven to set things right.

The people's sins were symbolically put on a goat's head,
bearing their iniquity into the wilderness it was led.
This transfer of guilt completing removal far and wide,
is a picture of Jesus, carrying our sin, He came and died.

In the temple the priest would sprinkle the east side of the mercy seat,
applying the blood of a bull to make clean, the atonement now complete.
This blood used to wash points to Jesus who cleanses our heart,
and foreshadows His return to Jerusalem, a new age it will start!

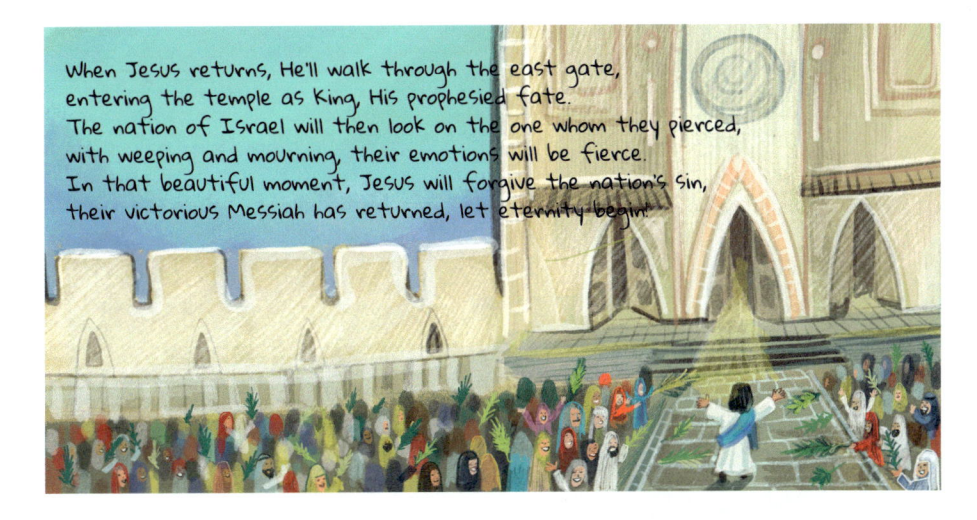

When Jesus returns, He'll walk through the east gate,
entering the temple as King, His prophesied fate.
The nation of Israel will then look on the one whom they pierced,
with weeping and mourning, their emotions will be fierce.
In that beautiful moment, Jesus will forgive the nation's sin,
their victorious Messiah has returned, let eternity begin!

What is the Day of Atonement?

The Day of Atonement, also known as Yom Kippur, marks the culmination or end of the 10 Days of Awe and is considered the holiest day of the Jewish year. The word kippur means covering, or atonement. God becoming one with His people was always His desire, and this special day of sacrifice and forgiveness of sins was designed to help achieve that. We can see where the Lord ordains this day in Leviticus 23:

"And the LORD spoke to Moses, saying: "Also the tenth day of this seventh month shall be the Day of Atonement. It shall be a holy convocation for you; you shall afflict your souls, and offer an offering made by fire to the LORD. And you shall do no work on that same day, for it is the Day of Atonement, to make atonement for you before the LORD your God. For any person who is not afflicted in soul on that same day shall be cut off from his people. And any person who does any work on that same day, that person I will destroy from among his people. You shall do no manner of work; it shall be a statute forever throughout your generations in all your dwellings. It shall be to you a Sabbath of solemn rest, and you shall afflict your souls; on the ninth day of the month at evening, from evening to evening, you shall celebrate your Sabbath." Leviticus 23:26-32

Take a look at the very first Yom Kippur. Read Exodus 32:

"Now when the people saw that Moses delayed coming down from the mountain, the people gathered together to Aaron, and said to him, "Come, make us gods that shall go before us; for as for this Moses, the man who brought us up out of the land of Egypt, we do not know what has become of him."

And Aaron said to them, "Break off the golden earrings which are in the ears of your wives, your sons, and your daughters, and bring them to me." So all the people broke off the golden earrings which were in their ears, and brought them to Aaron. And he received the gold from their hand, and he fashioned it with an engraving tool, and made a molded calf.

Then they said, "This is your god, O Israel, that brought you out of the land of Egypt!"

So when Aaron saw it, he built an altar before it. And Aaron made a proclamation and said, "Tomorrow is a feast to the Lord." Then they rose early on the next day, offered burnt offerings, and brought peace offerings; and the people sat down to eat and drink, and rose up to play.

And the Lord said to Moses, "Go, get down! For your people whom you brought out of the land of Egypt have corrupted themselves. They have turned aside quickly out of the way which I commanded them. They have made themselves a molded calf, and worshiped it and sacrificed to it, and said, 'This is your god, O Israel, that brought you out of the land of Egypt!' " And the Lord said to Moses, "I have seen this people, and indeed it is a stiff-necked people! Now therefore, let Me alone, that My wrath may burn hot against them and I may consume them. And I will make of you a great nation."

Then Moses pleaded with the Lord his God, and said: "Lord, why does Your wrath burn hot against Your people whom You have brought out of the land of Egypt with great power and with a mighty hand? Why should the Egyptians speak, and say, 'He brought them out to harm them, to kill them in the mountains, and to consume them from the face of the earth'? Turn from Your fierce wrath, and relent from this harm to Your people. Remember Abraham, Isaac, and Israel, Your servants, to whom You swore by Your own self, and said to them, 'I will multiply your descendants as the stars of heaven; and all this land that I have spoken of I give to your descendants, and they shall inherit it forever.' " So the Lord relented from the harm which He said He would do to His people.

And Moses turned and went down from the mountain, and the two tablets of the Testimony were in his hand. The tablets were written on both sides; on the one side and on the other they were written. Now the tablets were the work of God, and the writing was the writing of God engraved on the tablets.

And when Joshua heard the noise of the people as they shouted, he said to Moses, "There is a noise of war in the camp."

But he said:
"It is not the noise of the shout of victory,
Nor the noise of the cry of defeat,
But the sound of singing I hear."

So it was, as soon as he came near the camp, that he saw the calf and the dancing. So Moses' anger became hot, and he cast the tablets out of his hands and broke them at the foot of the mountain.

Then he took the calf which they had made, burned it in the fire, and ground it to powder; and he scattered it on the water and made the children of Israel drink it. And Moses said to Aaron, "What did this people do to you that you have brought so great a sin upon them?"

So Aaron said, "Do not let the anger of my lord become hot. You know the people, that they are set on evil. For they said to me, 'Make us gods that shall go before us; as for this Moses, the man who brought us out of the land of Egypt, we do not know what has become of him.' And I said to them, 'Whoever has any gold, let them break it off.' So they gave it to me, and I cast it into the fire, and this calf came out."

Now when Moses saw that the people were unrestrained (for Aaron had not restrained them, to their shame among their enemies), then Moses stood in the entrance of the camp, and said, "Whoever is on the Lord's side—come to me!" And all the sons of Levi gathered themselves together to him. And he said to them, "Thus says the Lord God of Israel: 'Let every man put his sword on his side, and go in and out from entrance to entrance throughout the camp, and let every man kill his brother, every man his companion, and every man his neighbor.' " So the sons of Levi did according to the word of Moses. And about three thousand men of the people fell that day. Then Moses said, "Consecrate yourselves today to the Lord, that He may bestow on you a blessing this day, for every man has opposed his son and his brother."

Now it came to pass on the next day that Moses said to the people, "You have committed a great sin. So now I will go up to the Lord; perhaps I can make atonement for your sin." Then Moses returned to the Lord and said, "Oh, these people have committed a great sin, and have made for themselves a god of gold! Yet now, if You will forgive their sin—but if not, I pray, blot me out of Your book which You have written."

And the Lord said to Moses, "Whoever has sinned against Me, I will blot him out of My book. Now therefore, go, lead the people to the place of which I have spoken to you. Behold, My Angel shall go before you. Nevertheless, in the day when I visit for punishment, I will visit punishment upon them for their sin."

So the Lord plagued the people because of what they did with the calf which Aaron made."

The first Yom Kippur took place when Moses came down from the mountain with the 10 Commandments and found the Israelites worshipping a golden calf which Aaron had made. In Moses' anger, he breaks the tablets, which symbolizes Israel breaking the covenant which the Lord had just made with them. Moses pleads with the Lord to not consume and destroy them and seeks to make atonement for their sin.

We then see later in the book of Exodus the Lord giving Israel the model of the Tabernacle of Meeting with the outer court, inner court and Holy of Holies. The Lord lays out instructions for how sacrifices would be performed to make atonement for sin. Yom Kippur was the one day each year that the high priest could enter the Holy of Holies to make atonement for the people's sin and ask for God's forgiveness on behalf of all the people of Israel.

Throughout the year, the Tabernacle absorbed all the sins of the people in sacrifice after sacrifice, day after day. Yom Kippur is like pushing the "reset" button – cleansing the place from all the sins of the people over the year and going back to zero.

On Yom Kippur, the high priest was required to take off his typical glorious robes and exchange them for simple white linen garments in order to go into the Holy of Holies. The white was to symbolize the holiness of the day and God wiping away the people's sins. This was a beautiful foreshadowing of Jesus, our great high priest putting aside His robes of heavenly splendor and putting on human flesh to become one of us.

God gives incredibly detailed instructions to the people for how they are supposed to perform sacrifices. We see this laid out in Leviticus 16. Read Leviticus 16:

"Now the Lord spoke to Moses after the death of the two sons of Aaron, when they offered profane fire before the Lord, and died; and the Lord said to Moses: "Tell Aaron your brother not to come at just any time into the Holy Place inside the veil, before the mercy seat which is on the ark, lest he die; for I will appear in the cloud above the mercy seat.

"Thus Aaron shall come into the Holy Place: with the blood of a young bull as a sin offering, and of a ram as a burnt offering. He shall put the holy linen tunic and the linen trousers on his body; he shall be girded with a linen sash, and with the linen turban he shall be attired. These are holy garments. Therefore he shall wash his body in water, and put them on.

And he shall take from the congregation of the children of Israel two kids of the goats as a sin offering, and one ram as a burnt offering.

"Aaron shall offer the bull as a sin offering, which is for himself, and make atonement for himself and for his house. He shall take the two goats and present them before the Lord at the door of the tabernacle of meeting. Then Aaron shall cast lots for the two goats: one lot for the Lord and the other lot for the scapegoat. And Aaron shall bring the goat on which the Lord's lot fell, and offer it as a sin offering. But the goat on which the lot fell to be the scapegoat shall be presented alive before the Lord, to make atonement upon it, and to let it go as the scapegoat into the wilderness.

"And Aaron shall bring the bull of the sin offering, which is for himself, and make atonement for himself and for his house, and shall kill the bull as the sin offering which is for himself. Then he shall take a censer full of burning coals of fire from the altar before the Lord, with his hands full of sweet incense beaten fine, and bring it inside the veil. And he shall put the incense on the fire before the Lord, that the cloud of incense may cover the mercy seat that is on the Testimony, lest he die. He shall take some of the blood of the bull and sprinkle it with his finger on the mercy seat on the east side; and before the mercy seat he shall sprinkle some of the blood with his finger seven times.

"Then he shall kill the goat of the sin offering, which is for the people, bring its blood inside the veil, do with that blood as he did with the blood of the bull, and sprinkle it on the mercy seat and before the mercy seat. So he shall make atonement for the Holy Place, because of the uncleanness of the children of Israel, and because of their transgressions, for all their sins; and so he shall do for the tabernacle of meeting which remains among them in the midst of their uncleanness. There shall be no man in the tabernacle of meeting when he goes in to make atonement in the Holy Place, until he comes out, that he may make atonement for himself, for his household, and for all the assembly of Israel. And he shall go out to the altar that is before the Lord, and make atonement for it, and shall take some of the blood of the bull and some of the blood of the goat, and put it on the horns of the altar all around. Then he shall sprinkle some of the blood on it with his finger seven times, cleanse it, and consecrate it from the uncleanness of the children of Israel.

"And when he has made an end of atoning for the Holy Place, the tabernacle of meeting, and the altar, he shall bring the live goat. Aaron shall lay both his hands on the head of the live goat, confess over it all the iniquities of the children of Israel, and all their transgressions, concerning all their sins, putting them on the head of the goat, and shall send it away into the wilderness by the hand of a suitable man. The goat shall bear on itself all their iniquities to an uninhabited land; and he shall release the goat in the wilderness.

"Then Aaron shall come into the tabernacle of meeting, shall take off the linen garments which he put on when he went into the Holy Place, and shall leave them there. And he shall wash his body with water in a holy place, put on his garments, come out and offer his burnt offering and the burnt offering of the people, and make atonement for himself and for the people. The fat of the sin offering he shall burn on the altar. And he who released the goat as the scapegoat shall wash his clothes and bathe his body in water, and afterward he may come into the camp. The bull for the sin offering and the goat for the sin offering, whose blood was brought in to make atonement in the Holy Place, shall be carried outside the camp. And they shall burn in the fire their skins, their flesh, and their offal. Then he who burns them shall wash his clothes and bathe his body in water, and afterward he may come into the camp.

"This shall be a statute forever for you: In the seventh month, on the tenth day of the month, you shall afflict your souls, and do no work at all, whether a native of your own country or a stranger who dwells among you. For on that day the priest shall make atonement for you, to cleanse you, that you may be clean from all your sins before the Lord. It is a sabbath of solemn rest for you, and you shall afflict your souls. It is a statute forever. And the priest, who is anointed and consecrated to minister as priest in his father's place, shall make atonement, and put on the linen clothes, the holy garments; then he shall make atonement for the Holy Sanctuary, and he shall make atonement for the tabernacle of meeting and for the altar, and he shall make atonement for the priests and for all the people of the assembly. This shall be an everlasting statute for you, to make atonement for the children of Israel, for all their sins, once a year." And he did as the Lord commanded Moses."

It's amazing all of the prophetic details that were in the instructions from the Lord; the incense offered before the Lord was a foreshadowing of the prayers of the saints that ascend before the throne of God (Revelation 5:8). The blood of the bull sprinkled on the east side of the Mercy Seat is a foreshadowing of Jesus whose blood redeemed us in His mercy. The east side is significant as Jesus will enter through the Eastern Gate of the Temple when He returns, and the blood being sprinkled seven times symbolizes the number of completion.

We see the sins and iniquity of the people transferred to a goat which is then sent into the wilderness. This is a beautiful picture of how the Lord removes our sins as far as the east is from the west. Finally, the high priest washing himself is a picture of the renewal of our baptism and the way the Lord washes us clean of our sins.

So how does this all point to Jesus' final return and the future redemption of Israel?

Take a look at Zechariah 3:6-10:
Then the Angel of the LORD admonished Joshua, saying, "Thus says the LORD of hosts: 'If you will walk in My ways, and if you will keep My command, then you shall also judge My house, and likewise have charge of My courts; I will give you places to walk among these who stand here. 'Hear, O Joshua, the high priest, you and your companions who sit before you, for they are a wondrous sign; for behold, I am bringing forth My Servant the BRANCH. For behold, the stone that I have laid before Joshua: upon the stone are seven eyes. Behold, I will engrave its inscription,' says the LORD of hosts, 'and I will remove the iniquity of that land in one day. In that day,' says the LORD of hosts, 'Everyone will invite his neighbor under his vine and under his fig tree.' "

And Zechariah 12:10-14:
"And I will pour on the house of David and on the inhabitants of Jerusalem the Spirit of grace and supplication; then they will look on Me whom they pierced. Yes, they will mourn for Him as one mourns for his only son, and grieve for Him as one grieves for a firstborn. In that day there shall be a great mourning in Jerusalem, like the mourning at Hadad Rimmon in the plain of Megiddo. And the land shall mourn, every family by itself: the family of the house of David by itself, and their wives by themselves; the family of the house of Nathan by itself, and their wives by themselves; the family of the house of Levi by itself, and their wives by themselves; the family of Shimei by itself, and their wives by themselves; all the families that remain, every family by itself, and their wives by themselves."

These passages in Zechariah tell us of the future redemption of Israel that will happen in a day. We know Jesus has made atonement for our sins to be clean, pure and one with God again through his death, burial and resurrection. Zechariah prophesies that there will be a nationwide realization in Israel of the one that they pierced and there will be mourning and grieving. On the final Yom Kippur when Jesus returns He will remove the sin and iniquity of Israel, they will look on the one they have pierced, mourn and lament and cry out to Him and He, Jesus will redeem Israel.

Today, the way Yom Kippur is celebrated is far from the Biblical mandate for Yom Kippur. Many Jews who aren't even religious or devout attend services on Yom Kippur much like many people who go to church services on Christmas aren't wholeheartedly following Jesus.

The Jewish people today believe that on Yom Kippur God decides each person's fate, so Jews are encouraged to make amends and ask forgiveness for sins committed during the past year. Yom Kippur is observed with a 25 hour fast and a special service. The Jewish people believe that during the 10 Days of Awe leading up to Yom Kippur the Lord judges them and inscribes the names of the righteous in the "Book of Life" and condemns the wicked to death. People who fall between the two categories have until Yom Kippur to perform "teshuva" which means repentance. So, if you are an observant Jew you will spend the days leading up to Yom Kippur in prayer, doing good deeds, reflecting on past mistakes and making amends with others.

This is a time where we can specifically be praying that they eyes of Jewish people are opened to the reality of who Jesus is, what He accomplished on the cross and that He is coming back again.

Feast of Tabernacles

A reminder of Israel's nomadic living in tents,
the seventh feast of all, the pinnacle of events!
To recall the intense times in the desert though temporary,
as an engagement between a man and woman to marry.
A relationship was forged between God as His people the Bride,
a picture of eternal commitment, knowing He'll always provide.

God calls His people to tabernacle for one week each year,
a reminder of short-lived camps in the desert, that's clear.
A sukkah is built, a makeshift house of branches and sticks,
symbolizing the chuppah, a Jewish wedding cover affixed.

For eight days in all the people celebrate and feast,
it all points to Jesus - our Savior, Bridegroom, High Priest.
This final celebration makes things eternally complete,
the marriage of the Bride with the Lamb will be forever sweet!

What is the Feast of Tabernacles?

The Feast of Tabernacles, or Sukkot, is a reminder of Israel's wandering in the desert dwelling in tents. The word sukkot means "tabernacles" or "booths". It is the seventh and final Biblical feast mandated by the Lord and brings completeness. It is a reminder of God's covenant with His people and the future picture of oneness when the Lamb returns and marries His bride.

Take a look at where the Lord mandates this feast in Scripture in Leviticus 23:34-44:

"Speak to the children of Israel, saying: 'The fifteenth day of this seventh month shall be the Feast of Tabernacles for seven days to the Lord. On the first day there shall be a holy convocation. You shall do no customary work on it. For seven days you shall offer an offering made by fire to the Lord. On the eighth day you shall have a holy convocation, and you shall offer an offering made by fire to the Lord. It is a sacred assembly, and you shall do no customary work on it.

'These are the feasts of the Lord which you shall proclaim to be holy convocations, to offer an offering made by fire to the Lord, a burnt offering and a grain offering, a sacrifice and drink offerings, everything on its day— besides the Sabbaths of the Lord, besides your gifts, besides all your vows, and besides all your freewill offerings which you give to the Lord.

'Also on the fifteenth day of the seventh month, when you have gathered in the fruit of the land, you shall keep the feast of the Lord for seven days; on the first day there shall be a sabbath-rest, and on the eighth day a sabbath-rest. And you shall take for yourselves on the first day the fruit of beautiful trees, branches of palm trees, the boughs of leafy trees, and willows of the brook; and you shall rejoice before the Lord your God for seven days. You shall keep it as a feast to the Lord for seven days in the year. It shall be a statute forever in your generations. You shall celebrate it in the seventh month. You shall dwell in booths for seven days. All who are native Israelites shall dwell in booths, that your generations may know that I made the children of Israel dwell in booths when I brought them out of the land of Egypt: I am the Lord your God.' "

So Moses declared to the children of Israel the feasts of the Lord."

We can see in this passage God calling His people to live in makeshift homes for a week to help the people remember this particular part of their journey with Him. The desert times were intense but temporary, and a very special time of forging the relationship between God and His people. Jesus celebrated this feast and used it to reveal His messianic identity as both the living water and the light of the world during the "water libation" and "illumination ceremonies."

During the water libation ceremony the temple priests gathered a pitcher of water from the pool of Siloam and poured it out on the altar inside the Temple. The pouring out of the water expressed Israel's hope for future rains to produce an abundant harvest. However at the time of Jesus, Israel was spiritually destitute. They were living under Roman rule. Even the Holy of Holies was empty and dry. This moment in the feast wasn't just a cry for physical rain, but a desperate cry that God would pour out his spirit - the 'living water' they longed for.

"On the last day, that great day of the feast, Jesus stood and cried out, saying, "If anyone thirsts, let him come to Me and drink. He who believes in Me, as the Scripture has said, out of his heart will flow rivers of living water." But this He spoke concerning the Spirit, whom those believing in Him would receive; for the Holy Spirit was not yet given, because Jesus was not yet glorified." John 7:37-39

The 'Illumination of the Temple' was another important ceremony during the feast. It involved the lighting of four golden oil-fed lamps in the Court of Women. These lamps were lit in the Temple at night to remind Israel of the pillar of fire that had led them in their wilderness journey. The light was so bright that it is said to have illuminated the entire city.

This ceremony was also a reminder that God had promised to send a light to renew Israel's glory, release them from bondage, and restore their joy. This was the context for Jesus' declaration in John 8:12: Then Jesus spoke to them again, saying, "I am the light of the world. He who follows Me shall not walk in darkness, but have the light of life."

The final picture of this feast is that of a wedding; we can think about the time Israel had in the wilderness with God as an engagement period. There are so many amazing parallels between a Jewish wedding and the Feast of Tabernacles.

Sukkot is the final feast where God and man can at last move in together, like a newly-wed couple who have been longing for complete union. "He brought me to the banqueting house, and his banner over me was love." Song of Solomon 2:4.

In a Jewish wedding ceremony, the bride and groom stand under the chuppah, a symbol of the bridegroom's permanent and real home. The bride in Song of Songs talks about being invited into her love's chambers. Like a sukkah, the chuppa is a temporary shelter symbolizing a home, where there is great rejoicing and intimate fellowship. The word chuppah means covering or protection, and acts as a symbolic roof, covering the couple who are getting married. It is where the legal business of betrothal takes place, and symbolizes the home of the groom, into which the bride is welcomed.

In Jewish weddings, rejoicing is taken very seriously. This is also true with the Feast of Sukkot. It is the only feast in which we are actually commanded to rejoice. Read Deuteronomy 16:14-16:

"And you shall rejoice in your feast, you and your son and your daughter, your male servant and your female servant and the Levite, the stranger and the fatherless and the widow, who are within your gates. Seven days you shall keep a sacred feast to the Lord your God in the place which the Lord chooses, because the Lord your God will bless you in all your produce and in all the work of your hands, so that you surely rejoice.

"Three times a year all your males shall appear before the Lord your God in the place which He chooses: at the Feast of Unleavened Bread, at the Feast of Weeks, and at the Feast of Tabernacles; and they shall not appear before the Lord empty-handed."

Similarly, the cloud that protected the Israelites by day during their desert years also parallels the chuppa canopy. We know a wedding is the pinnacle of rejoicing and this is what Sukkot is all pointing to – the ultimate wedding feast of the Lamb and His spotless bride which we see prophesied in Revelation 21:1-5:

"Now I saw a new heaven and a new earth, for the first heaven and the first earth had passed away. Also, there was no more sea. Then I, John, saw the holy city, New Jerusalem, coming down out of heaven from God, prepared as a bride adorned for her husband.

And I heard a loud voice from heaven saying, "Behold, the tabernacle of God is with men, and He will dwell with them, and they shall be His people. God Himself will be with them and be their God. And God will wipe away every tear from their eyes; there shall be no more death, nor sorrow, nor crying. There shall be no more pain, for the former things have passed away." Then He who sat on the throne said, "Behold, I make all things new." And He said to me, "Write, for these words are true and faithful."

And...did you know we will be celebrating the Feast of Tabernacles for 1,000 years during the Millennial Reign of Jesus? Check out Zechariah 14:16-19:

"And it shall come to pass that everyone who is left of all the nations which came against Jerusalem shall go up from year to year to worship the King, the Lord of hosts, and to keep the Feast of Tabernacles. And it shall be that whichever of the families of the earth do not come up to Jerusalem to worship the King, the Lord of hosts, on them there will be no rain. If the family of Egypt will not come up and enter in, they shall have no rain; they shall receive the plague with which the Lord strikes the nations who do not come up to keep the Feast of Tabernacles. This shall be the punishment of Egypt and the punishment of all the nations that do not come up to keep the Feast of Tabernacles."

Celebrating the Fall Feasts
Book Suggestions

Ages 0+
- What Do You See? On Rosh Hashannah & Yom Kippur   By: Bracha Goetz
- What Do You See? On Sukkos   By: Bracha Goetz
- Rosh Hashannah is Coming   By: Tracy Newman
- Sukkot is Coming   By: Tracy Newman

Ages 3+
- The Fall Feasts   By: Jessica AcMoody
- Jesus Calling Bible Storybook   By: Sarah Young
    - A Golden Calf (p.74-75)
    - John's Dream (p.252-256)

Ages 5+
- The Jesus Storybook Bible   By: Sally Lloyd-Jones
    - A Dream of Heaven (p.342-349)

Ages 8+
- The Action Bible   By: Sergio Cariello
    - A Golden Calf (p.166-171)
    - The Tent of Meeting (p.172-175)
    - Sacrifice and Blessing (p.176-177)
    - The Final Days (p.816-817)

Activities

Feast of Trumpets
Make your own shofars
Grab a few paper towel tubes to make your own shofars with. You can decorate them with markers, ribbons, paint, whatever miscellaneous art supplies you might have on hand that you want to use. Be creative and enjoy making your own unique shofar. As you read through "The Fall Feasts" book have your kids listen for the word "trumpet" and sound their shofar each time you read the word "trumpet".

Eat a trumpet shaped snack (Bugels or ice cream cones)
Whip up a quick snack for your kids with a trumpet shaped go-to like Bugels or ice cream cones. The ice cream cones could be filled with yogurt and fruit and then topped with sprinkles or chocolate chips, you could fill them with cupcake batter and bake them in the oven or fill with a mixture of chopped bananas, any nut butter and top with chia, hemp or flax seeds.

Day of Atonement
Learn about Teshuva
Teshuva is repentance. Talk with your children about what repentance is and what it looks like to live a lifestyle of repentance before God. Spend some time as a family praying together. Ask God to search your hearts and show you where He is calling you to repent and turn back to Him. Ask Him to help each of you by the Holy Spirit to live wholeheartedly for Him.

Feast of Tabernacles
Eat Apples & Honey
One of the foods traditionally eaten at the Feast of Tabernacles (Rosh Hashanah) is apples and honey. Apples dipped in honey is a symbol of hope for the new year. Apples are symbolic of the Garden of Eden and honey is symbolic of the sweetness of life.

Have a camp out

What better way to commemorate the Israelites time in the wilderness tabernacling with God than to have a camp out? Whether it's in your backyard or you go on a special trip somewhere the week of Sukkot, enjoy sleeping under the stars! If sleeping outside isn't your thing then set up a tent in your backyard and enjoy reading books in it during the day. Kids love playing in tents and maybe they'll want to have nap time out there.

Build a Sukkah

In Scripture God commands His people to build a sukkah or makeshift tabernacle for one week each year. This temporary shelter constructed for the week of Sukkot is a place eat meals. It's traditional for Jewish families to invite relatives and friends over for dinner each night or go to someone else's house for a meal each night. Who might you invite over for a meal? A quick internet search will give you several ideas for how you could build your sukkah and what it might look like. Have fun and be creative!

Connections Between Exodus and Revelation

Did you know that almost every plague in Exodus is reflected in Revelation in some way?

In Exodus God meets face to face with Moses and calls Moses to lead the people into freedom in the wilderness to worship and hold a feast to the Lord. But Pharaoh will not let the people go. His heart is hard and will not change, and his heart is hardened even more by the Lord with each plague God sends. Each plague sent upon Egypt is to display the mighty wonders of God and bring God's people one step closer to feasting with the Lord in the wilderness.

Likewise, each of the seal, trumpet and bowl judgments in Revelation in the last days are an opportunity for believers and those who do not yet know the Lord to humble themselves before God and turn towards the Him. The judgments of the Lord are righteous and are also His mercy as He extends one last chance for the Church and humanity to turn to Him with their whole hearts before the final feast of all feasts – the marriage of the Lamb and the Bride.

Check out what Psalm 19 tells us about embracing the judgments of the Lord:
"The fear of the LORD is clean, enduring forever; the judgments of the LORD are true and righteous altogether. More to be desired are they than gold, yea, than much fine gold; sweeter also than honey and the honeycomb. Moreover by them Your servant is warned, and in keeping them there is great reward." Psalm 19:9-11

Let's take a look at the connections between the plagues in Exodus and the judgments in Revelation:

Connection #1 - Waters turned to blood
Read Exodus 7:14-25 – 1st plague
Read Revelation 8:8-9 – 2nd trumpet judgment
Read Revelation 16:3-7 – 2nd/3rd bowl judgments

Connection #2 – Frogs
Read Exodus 8:1-15 – 2nd plague
Read Revelation 16:12-16 – 6th bowl judgment

Connection #3 – Pestilence
Read Exodus 9:1-7 – 5th plague
Read Revelation 6:7-8 – 4th seal judgment

Connection #4 – Boils
Read Exodus 9:8-12 – 6th plague
Read Revelation 16:2 – 1st bowl judgment

Connection #5 – Hail & Fire
Read Exodus 9:13-35 – 7th plague
Read Revelation 8:7 – 1st trumpet judgment

Connection #6 - Locusts
Read Exodus 10:1-20 – 8th plague
Read Revelation 9:1-11 – 5th trumpet judgment

Connection #7 – Darkness
Read Exodus 10:21-29 – 9th plague
Read Revelation 16:10-11 – 5th bowl judgment

Just as the plagues of Exodus were literal plagues, so too will the judgments of Revelation be in the last days leading up to the return of Jesus. Many in the Church have been wrongly taught about the judgments of Revelation, either writing the whole book off as symbolic or taught to believe that followers of Jesus will be raptured before any of the judgments touch the earth. It is clear from Scripture that the rapture or gathering of believers sealed by God happens at the last trumpet:

"Immediately after the tribulation of those days the sun will be darkened, and the moon will not give its light; the stars will fall from heaven, and the powers of the heavens will be shaken. Then the sign of the Son of Man will appear in heaven, and then all the tribes of the earth will mourn, and they will see the Son of Man coming on the clouds of heaven with power and great glory. And He will send His angels with a great sound of a trumpet, and they will gather together His elect from the four winds, from one end of heaven to the other." Matthew 24:29-31

"Behold, I tell you a mystery: We shall not all sleep, but we shall all be changed— in a moment, in the twinkling of an eye, at the last trumpet. For the trumpet will sound, and the dead will be raised incorruptible, and we shall be changed." 1 Corinthians 15:51-52

"For the Lord Himself will descend from heaven with a shout, with the voice of an archangel, and with the trumpet of God. And the dead in Christ will rise first. Then we who are alive and remain shall be caught up together with them in the clouds to meet the Lord in the air. And thus we shall always be with the Lord. Therefore comfort one another with these words." 1 Thessalonians 4:16-18.

The Church will be present on the earth as a majority of the judgments unfold and touch the earth. So, what is the role of the Church in the last days? We can see a mandate from the Lord laid out in Joel 2:

Repent – rend your heart: Joel 2:12-14
"Now, therefore," says the Lord, "Turn to Me with all your heart, with fasting, with weeping, and with mourning." So rend your heart, and not your garments; return to the Lord your God, for He is gracious and merciful, slow to anger, and of great kindness; and He relents from doing harm. Who knows if He will turn and relent, and leave a blessing behind Him— a grain offering and a drink offering for the Lord your God?

Gather – consecrate a fast: Joel 2:15-16
"Blow the trumpet in Zion, consecrate a fast, call a sacred assembly; gather the people, sanctify the congregation, assemble the elders, gather the children and nursing babes; let the bridegroom go out from his chamber, and the bride from her dressing room."

Pray – come into the place of prayer: Joel 2:17
"Let the priests, who minister to the Lord, weep between the porch and the altar; let them say, "Spare Your people, O Lord, and do not give Your heritage to reproach, that the nations should rule over them. Why should they say among the peoples, 'Where is their God?'"

In the last days the Church that will become the Bride is called to become pure and spotless, preparing for her wedding day to the Lamb at the end of the age. The final place where the Lamb and Bride rule and reign together will be the hill of the Lord or Zion – yes, literal Mount Zion in Jerusalem. We can see this laid out in Psalm 24:

"The earth is the Lord's, and all its fullness, the world and those who dwell therein. For He has founded it upon the seas, and established it upon the waters.

Who may ascend into the hill of the Lord? Or who may stand in His holy place? He who has clean hands and a pure heart, who has not lifted up his soul to an idol, nor sworn deceitfully. He shall receive blessing from the Lord, and righteousness from the God of his salvation. This is Jacob, the generation of those who seek Him, who seek Your face. Selah

Lift up your heads, O you gates! And be lifted up, you everlasting doors! And the King of glory shall come in. Who is this King of glory? The Lord strong and mighty, the Lord mighty in battle. Lift up your heads, O you gates! Lift up, you everlasting doors! And the King of glory shall come in. Who is this King of glory? The Lord of hosts, He is the King of glory. Selah

Take some time to sit before the Lord and ask Him to lead you by His Spirit in these things; to repent, gather and pray with other believers.

"But the hour is coming, and now is, when the true worshipers will worship the Father in spirit and truth; for the Father is seeking such to worship Him. God is Spirit, and those who worship Him must worship in spirit and truth." John 4:23-24

Then let His Spirit empower you to be a witness - Matthew 28:18-20, knowing He will be with you and lead you "even to the end of the age."

About the author...

Jessica AcMoody is a wife and stay at home mother of two. Through a small web based ministry she enjoys creating and sharing resources for families to grow together in the Lord.

For a decade, before becoming a mother, she was an urban Christian school educator. Serving first as an elementary school teacher at Tree of Life School in Kalamazoo, MI and then as elementary school principal and founder of River of Life School in Benton Harbor, MI.

You can follow her ministry page "Elemental Faith" on both Facebook and Instagram for more resources and Bible-based content.

About the illustrator...

Ira Baykovska is a children's book illustrator and a mom of two beautiful girls.

Ira has been drawing for as long as she can remember and sometimes cannot believe that this hobby has become her life-long career.

She has been working as a freelance illustrator since 2014 and has illustrated more than 20 books for kids. Ira has a degree in Graphic Design and currently lives and works in Lviv, Ukraine.

Visit Ira's website www.baykovska.com

Other titles by the author...

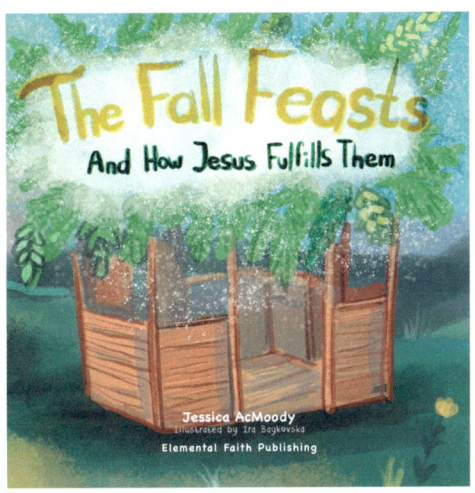

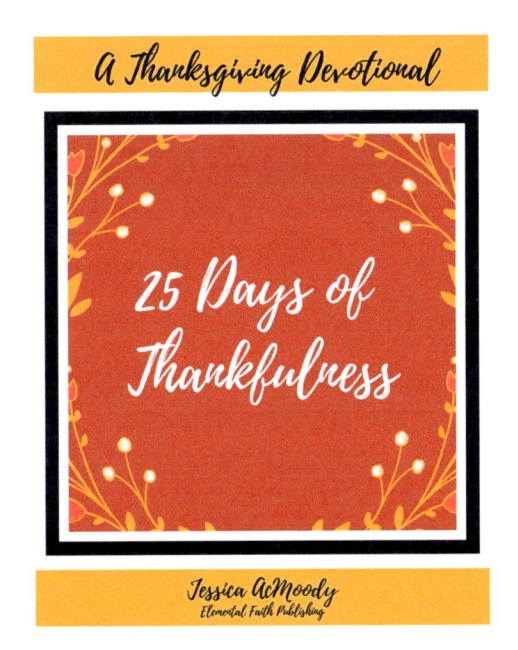

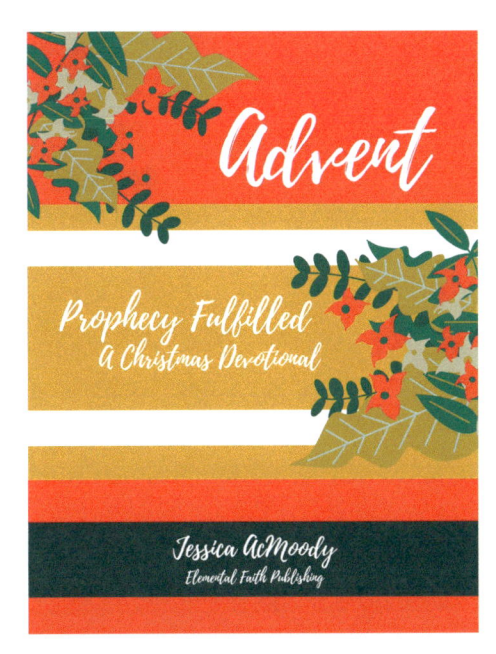

- **The Spring Feasts And How Jesus Fulfilled Them** — Jessica AcMoody, Illustrated by Ira Baykovska, Elemental Faith Publishing
- **The Feast of Weeks: When the Holy Spirit Came** — Jessica AcMoody, Illustrated by Ira Baykovska, Elemental Faith Publishing
- **The Fall Feasts And How Jesus Fulfills Them** — Jessica AcMoody, Illustrated by Ira Baykovska, Elemental Faith Publishing
- **A Thanksgiving Devotional: 25 Days of Thankfulness** — Jessica AcMoody, Elemental Faith Publishing
- **Advent: Prophecy Fulfilled — A Christmas Devotional** — Jessica AcMoody, Elemental Faith Publishing

Order on Amazon or email:
elementalfaithpublishing@gmail.com

Made in the USA
Columbia, SC
28 April 2025